Cambridge Elements

Elements in Critical Heritage Studies
edited by
Kristian Kristiansen
University of Gothenburg
Michael Rowlands
UCL

A CHINESE DISCOURSE OF HERITAGE

Song Hou
Shantou University

Shaftesbury Road, Cambridge CB2 8EA, United Kingdom

One Liberty Plaza, 20th Floor, New York, NY 10006, USA

477 Williamstown Road, Port Melbourne, VIC 3207, Australia

314–321, 3rd Floor, Plot 3, Splendor Forum, Jasola District Centre, New Delhi – 110025, India

103 Penang Road, #05–06/07, Visioncrest Commercial, Singapore 238467

Cambridge University Press is part of Cambridge University Press & Assessment, a department of the University of Cambridge.

We share the University's mission to contribute to society through the pursuit of education, learning and research at the highest international levels of excellence.

www.cambridge.org
Information on this title: www.cambridge.org/9781009495677

DOI: 10.1017/9781009495660

© Song Hou 2026

This publication is in copyright. Subject to statutory exception and to the provisions of relevant collective licensing agreements, no reproduction of any part may take place without the written permission of Cambridge University Press & Assessment.

When citing this work, please include a reference to the DOI 10.1017/9781009495660

First published 2026

A catalogue record for this publication is available from the British Library

ISBN 978-1-009-49567-7 Hardback
ISBN 978-1-009-49564-6 Paperback
ISSN 2632-7074 (online)
ISSN 2632-7066 (print)

Cambridge University Press & Assessment has no responsibility for the persistence or accuracy of URLs for external or third-party internet websites referred to in this publication and does not guarantee that any content on such websites is, or will remain, accurate or appropriate.

For EU product safety concerns, contact us at Calle de José Abascal, 56, 1°, 28003 Madrid, Spain, or email eugpsr@cambridge.org

A Chinese Discourse of Heritage

Elements in Critical Heritage Studies

DOI: 10.1017/9781009495660
First published online: January 2026

Song Hou
Shantou University
Author for correspondence: Song Hou, housong@stu.edu.cn

Abstract: This Element presents an alternative approach to critical heritage studies by attending to forgotten or transformed cultural, historical ideas of heritage. It focuses on the Chinese term *guji* (古迹 ancient traces or vestiges), perceived today as the same as the modern concept of cultural heritage. After a macroanalysis of how *guji* is understood differently in contemporary and historical China, it comes to cultural-historical discourse analysis of *guji* recorded in the local gazetteers of Quzhou from the 1500s to the 1920s, revealing its way of categorization as boundary negotiation, and cultural modes of meaning-making and remembering, either with or without physical remains or a verifiable site. After a holistic view of this Chinese discourse as reflected in a particular *guji*, it concludes with a philosophical lens to highlight the alternative existence of heritage in the word *guji* and the uses of heritage as the uses of language.

Keywords: history of heritage, discourse analysis, alternative Chinese concept, language, memory

© Song Hou 2026

ISBNs: 9781009495677 (HB), 9781009495646 (PB), 9781009495660 (OC)
ISSNs: 2632-7074 (online), 2632-7066 (print)

Contents

1 Introduction   1

2 *Guji* Present and *Guji* Past   13

3 What Can *Guji* Be? The Categorization and Boundary Negotiation of *Guji*   22

4 The Materiality/Physicality of *Guji*   35

5 *Guji* in a Holistic View   50

6 Concluding Remarks   56

References   62

1 Introduction

HERITAGE IS EVERYWHERE

Lowenthal 1998: 1, original capitalization

When David Lowenthal began his seminal work *The Heritage Crusade and the Spoils of History* some twenty years ago, he wrote this statement to critique the global heritage movement. Here, I borrow it, not only to mean that the heritage movement is more pervasive today and demands for more critical inquiries but also to summon greater diversity in heritage thinking, research, and practice. Indeed, heritage is everywhere, but people in different parts of the world may talk about, understand, and deal with it differently. This Element starts from the premise that heritage is not something out there but a meaning-making process and sociocultural practice; a key component is how discourse works to represent and construct what heritage is (not) and coerces how people perceive and act upon heritage (Smith 2006; Waterton 2010a; Wu & Hou 2015). I aim to accentuate that heritage (as) discourse is culturally saturated and should be diverse or diversified in relation to geography and time. For critical heritage scholars, searching for and rearticulating alternative cultural discourses of heritage that have been marginalized, devalued, or forgotten in the global heritage movement is equally, if not more, important than critiquing the dominant discourses to advance this new interdisciplinary field of inquiry.

In recent years, we have seen increasingly more research endeavors to explore alternative discourses of heritage, among which most are done from ethnographic and community-archaeological perspectives (e.g., Astudillo & Salazar 2024; Byrne 2014; De Jong & Rowlands 2007; Evans & Rowlands 2021; Onciul 2015; Rico 2016; Schmidt 2017; Yu & Mei 2024). This Element intends to showcase a different approach to critical heritage studies, one that turns our attention to forgotten or transformed discourses of heritage in their cultural-historical contexts. In other words, I advocate for an approach to researching and rearticulating cultural discourses of heritage in past times. As Harvey (2001) has pointed out, heritage is a human condition, rather than a modern movement starting from the nineteenth century or any other time. By analyzing how people write and make meaning of the past in the past, we can not only challenge the knowledge/power of the Western "Authorized Heritage Discourse" (AHD, Smith 2006) but also demonstrate how heritage might be conceptualized, categorized, communicated, and construed in different ways and with alternative cultural logics over time and across geographical areas.

This historical perspective on heritage (as) discourse is largely overlooked in current critical heritage scholarship. It is not that critical heritage researchers have little interest in history or historical materials. On the contrary, most of them do. Yet, rarely do they conduct discourse analysis of historical documents to rearticulate forgotten or substituted cultural ideas of heritage, or their underlying ways of thinking and valuing the past. As I will demonstrate, unpacking heritage discourse in history is genuinely beneficial to diversify heritage thinking, research, and practice. In China, this historical approach is particularly useful, if not indispensable. For one thing, China has a long history of dealing with sites and objects that we tend to call "heritage" today, yet its contemporary heritage policies and practices have been largely shaped by modern, Western discourses, the AHD in particular. Though the cry for rethinking and reformulating heritage becomes increasingly louder, Western-originated concepts, principles, and models of heritage practice are still mainstream. For another, China is extremely rich in historical documents, which provide data for us to find alternative cultural ways of conceptualizing, categorizing, and constructing what we today term heritage. My focus in this Element is on a Chinese cultural discourse – *guji* (古迹, ancient traces or vestiges) in historical times. *Guji* is putatively the first term that would come to mind if a Chinese person were asked for a counterpart to cultural heritage in their language (Hou 2019: 456; see also Li 2013). As will be shown, although this Chinese word is still widely in use, the meaning or idea it conveys has been subtly transformed by the Western, globalized discourse of heritage. My central task is to rearticulate how the Chinese, in times before their enthusiastic embrace of modern, Western historical consciousness and the World Heritage Movement, represented and made meaning of their *guji* for remembrance and responsive actions. *Guji* might include historic buildings, sites, and places that readily fall into the category of cultural heritage, as well as others that are hard to classify as heritage in its contemporary definition such as a tree or a stone (see section 3). I will first examine how *guji* is generally understood in China in the present era of "world heritage craze" (Yan 2018) and in historical times. This can be regarded as a macroanalysis of the Chinese *guji* discourse. Then, I come to the core of this treatise: a focused cultural-historical discourse analysis of *guji* in an ordinary Chinese heritage city, namely, Quzhou in the Zhejiang province.

This grounded historical inquiry into the *guji* discourse will help rearticulate Chinese cultural ways of meaning-making and remembering the past, which have been discarded, forgotten, or transformed while the country has embraced the modern historical consciousness and ethos of heritage conservation originating from Europe. It is thus both a critical project to challenge the AHD and other globalized heritage ways of thinking that construe commonsense knowledge of what heritage is and how it should be handled, and a constructive enterprise to promote dialogue and diversity regarding heritage from a Chinese cultural and historical perspective. In Harvey's (2024: 4) words, this Element presents a "more-than-critical" approach to heritage studies, as I will not only critique the dominant, authoritative discourses but also take "an invitational attitude towards alternative modes of being and doing." I can also say this approach reflects a Chinese cultural understanding of critical scholarship: being critical does not necessarily mean confronting, challenging, or deconstructing; acts of historicizing, exploring alternatives, or remaking can be critical as well (Hou & Wu 2015; Zhu 2024b; see also Hou & Wu 2017 for an alternative approach to critical discourse studies based on a case study of heritage in Quzhou).

Furthermore, this Element also contributes to advancing heritage discourse studies – a research line that integrates heritage studies and discourse studies, the history of heritage (particularly, the conceptual history, or history of ideas of heritage in China), and other pertinent interdisciplinary areas of scholarship, such as memory studies, historical geography, and Chinese studies. As Wu and Hou (2015) have pointed out, heritage discourse studies focus mostly on critiquing the authoritative, dominant, and globalized, by adopting various discourse analytical methods such as critical discourse analysis (Barry & Teron 2023; Smith 2006: chapter 3; Waterton 2010a; Waterton et al. 2006), Foucauldian discourse analysis (Melis & Chambers 2021; Wight 2016), multi-modal discourse analysis (Feng et al. 2017, 2018; Skrede & Andersen 2023; Waterton 2009, 2010b), and sociolinguistic discourse analysis (Coupland & Coupland 2014; Coupland et al. 2005), as well as a combination of discourse analysis with other methodological or epistemological perspectives (Angouri et al. 2017; Skrede 2020; Skrede & Hølleland 2018). However, discourse analytical perspectives and methods are much less frequently applied to explore alternative ways of talking about and thinking of what we today tend to call "heritage." To present a discourse analysis of an alternative concept of heritage from historical China, this Element intends to bridge historical and discourse studies of heritage, and to encourage cross-fertilization of these two subfields of heritage research. As I will show, rearticulating disregarded, forgotten cultural discourses of what is now termed "heritage," such as *guji*, in their pasts is a compelling approach to rethinking and reconstructing heritage.

Although historical research on heritage has been growing in recent years (e.g., Bloembergen & Eickhoff 2020; D'Agostino 2021; Falser 2020; Jokilehto 2017; Swenson 2013; Zhu 2024a), it remains a relatively underdeveloped subfield of heritage scholarship. Systematic studies in the conceptual history or history of ideas regarding heritage are even scarcer (but see Eriksen 2014; Wang 2017). It should be noted that many scholars have concerns over perceptions or understandings of heritage in historical times, yet their studies are concentrated on historical practices or ways of practicing what we now tend to call "heritage." (Gilman 2010: chapter 4; Wang 2020; Wang & Rowlands

2017; Zhu 2024a) These studies are better described as cultural or social histories of heritage. The current Element is intended to contribute to the conceptual history of heritage by explicating the Chinese notion of *guji*. Eriksen's (2014) historical inquiry into the evolution of such concepts as antiquity, monument, and cultural heritage in Nordic culture since the 18th century is a rare and laudable book-length contribution to this branch of heritage history. My work in this Element is more focused: It investigates one single Chinese cultural concept of heritage in an eastern Chinese city–Quzhou (衢州)– during the period from late imperial to mid Republican China, or, more precisely, from the 1500s to the 1920s. Wang Shu-li's (2017) historical exposition of the Chinese term *wenwu* (文物) is, perhaps, the most similar to my research. However, her study is rather general, without detailed analysis of specific historical texts. Adopting a discourse analytical approach, I attempt to unravel the disregarded cultural episteme and meaning-making apparatus of *guji*, hoping to facilitate heritage rethinking and dialogue in a more nuanced manner.

A Cultural-Historical Discourse Approach to Heritage

Discourse, as Foucault (1972: 49) states, consists of "practices which systematically form the objects of which they speak." Heritage can be viewed as such an object formed in and through discursive practices, primarily our words that speak of it. In this Element, I further highlight, following cultural discourse scholars, the embeddedness of discourse in culture. Shi-xu (2005, 2014), for example, theorizes discourse as cultural ways of speaking. As he writes:

> different cultures have different histories, conditions, problems, issues, aspirations, and so on. Consequently, the different cultural discourses which constitute them will have not only different objects of construction or topics, but also different categorizations, understandings, perspectives, evaluations, and so on. They make up different cultural worlds, so to speak. (Shi-xu 2005: 62)

Donal Carbaugh, another leading advocate of cultural discourse research, defines cultural discourse as "a historically transmitted expressive system of communication practices, of acts, events, and styles, which are composed of specific symbols, symbolic forms, norms, and their meanings" (2007: 169). Both of these scholars have pinpointed the link between cultural discourse and history. When studying cultural discourses of heritage, this link should be more accentuated. The reason for this is simple: Heritage is "historically transmitted" as well. What is more, as will be shown, careful investigations into history can lead us to see alternative ways of heritage conceptualization, categorization, communication, construction, and action, which should be transmitted yet are largely stigmatized, marginalized, or forgotten in the present climate of global heritage craze. Therefore, we need to approach history from a discourse perspective, particularly a cultural discourse perspective. That means studying history is not to trace historical facts, events, causes, or backgrounds but rather to look into the texts produced in the past and scrutinize how those texts construct what we tend to classify as "heritage" today.

That said, I am bringing to light a cultural-historical discourse approach to heritage. It grows out of my efforts in collaboration with colleagues in exploring alternative Chinese understandings of heritage (Hou 2019; Hou & Wu 2012, 2015; Hou et al. 2019). It is different from the established cultural approaches to discourse analysis, such as Shi-xu's "cultural discourse studies" (2005, 2015) and Carbaugh's "cultural discourse analysis" (1996, 2007) in that it focuses on historical rather than contemporary texts as its main data. The defining attribute of this approach is that it is simultaneously cultural and historical. That is, the researcher takes on a discursive perspective on history and a historical perspective on discourse. Following Foucault (1984) and White (1973, 1987), I see history as a form of narrative or discursive construction. Historical inquiries are not much about finding a systemic process of development or the causes for a present discourse (cf. Blommaert 2005: 37; Flowerdew 2012; Reisigl & Wodak 2015). Rather, they involve collecting and interpreting various texts produced in historical times and unpacking the meaning production, reality construction, and ways of remembering, valuing, and using what we today term "heritage" in the past. In other words, by probing into history, we come to understand the forgotten historical words and worlds, values and ways of valuing, and thoughts and modes of thinking about "heritage"; and we can attend to the divergences, ruptures, and transformations in how heritage is conceptualized, categorized, and coped with in different times. Such an approach will allow us to historicize present discourses of heritage in China and reflect upon their underlying ways of knowing and politics of the past.

Furthermore, this cultural-historical discourse approach to heritage will not rigidly follow any established discourse analytical framework to explain and interpret data, given that they are designed primarily for or based on the investigation of texts coded in modern languages, especially European languages (Shi-xu 2012). Nor will I attempt to set up a new discourse analytical framework claimed to be more applicable for examining texts in classical Chinese, which is impossible in the space this Element allows. Instead, some analytical strategies can be outlined here to serve as rough guidelines for cultural-historical discourse studies of heritage.

First, the beginning of this cultural-historical discourse approach is a set of commonly asked questions for undertaking discourse analysis:

(1) What is (not) said about "heritage" (in general terms or a specific instance) in the texts under investigation?
(2) How is the said articulated, and how is the unsaid concealed?
(3) What underlying meaning- and value-making may be sustained, and what ideology or cultural way of thinking may be significant in such forms of discursive representation of "heritage"?
(4) What social and cultural consequences and responses may such discursive representations of "heritage" bring forth?

Bearing these questions in mind, the researcher starts to read the textual data they have collected critically.

Second, the noticeable features in the textual data under inspection generally become the focal points for analysis. These features may be about content (topics, themes, categories, events) or form (linguistic-textual, intertextual, stylistic, rhetorical, generic, and so on) in representing "heritage." Analytical vocabularies from heritage studies, discourse and communication studies, and other relevant disciplines may be useful for describing those content or formal features, such as materiality, authenticity, site, emotion, and quotation.

Third, it is also important to interpret the meaning- or value-making process, discursive-constructing work, and cultural ways of thinking, doing, and being regarding "heritage" underlying the content and form of the historical texts under study. This interpretive procedure should involve careful examination of the local, cultural, and historical contexts in which the texts are produced. Furthermore, comparative and contrastive analysis with reference to the dominant, globalized discourses may be illuminating.

I should note that, when doing cultural-historical discourse analysis of "heritage," it is not always necessary to address every point mentioned in the commonly asked questions outlined previously, or to scrutinize every form or content feature identified in the textual data. Rather, the researcher selects the most salient features that serve their analytical purposes, as discourse analysts usually do. For example, the researcher may choose the thematic and some of the linguistic-textual features to analyze their data and then interpret how those features work to construct alternative heritage understandings and values.

This cultural-historical discourse approach is effective in rearticulating alternative understandings of heritage in cultural settings. For example, I have adopted this method to delineate the remembrance of trees as heritage in the city of Hangzhou during the Qing dynasty (1636–1911), revealing a fourfold meaning-making apparatus through which trees, physically existent or not, were rendered culturally significant for the remembrance of historical figures, place names, poetic writings, and exceptional landscapes. In this Element, my focus is Quzhou in the late imperial and mid Republican eras.

Quzhou as an Ordinary Chinese Heritage City: The Context and Texts

To study Chinese *guji* discourse, it would be useful to probe into a particular locality, apart from observations and analyses at macro levels. As Walsh states in his critical study of heritage representations in the United Kingdom, "What is necessary is a rearticulation of discourses based on *the locality*, a manageable context which permits the development of democratic discourse" (1992: 3; my emphasis). I chose the city of Quzhou as the locality to serve my objective of rearticulating a marginalized, forgotten Chinese cultural discourse of heritage, hoping to facilitate the development and dialogue between different heritage discourses. Nonetheless, I do not think there is one democratic discourse that is good for all. As is known, either democracy or discourse implies choice-making, that is, to select and foreground one among possible alternatives.

Situated in western Zhejiang (see Figure 1), Quzhou is about 230 kilometers northwest from the provincial capital Hangzhou, and about 400 kilometers southwest from the biggest Chinese city Shanghai. Like most Chinese cities, Quzhou has a long history to trace. According to local historiographies, it was first established as a county in 192 AD, called Xin'an (新安), which

Figure 1 A map of Zhejiang province emphasizing Quzhou.

was renamed Xin'an (信安) in 280. In 621, the prefecture of Quzhou was founded in the early Tang dynasty, with Xin'an County (信安县) being its prefectural seat (Shen et al. 2009: 7; Lin et al. 2009: 380). Some 250 years later, the city name Xin'an (信安) was changed to Xi'an (西安), which lasted until the end of imperial China. With the transition to the Republic of China in 1912, its name was altered to Qu County (衢县; Zheng 1984: 118, 121). The county of Xin'an, Xi'an or Qu shares roughly the same territory as the present Quzhou city. It is the regional scope this Element will focus on.

Quzhou is one among the 142 renowned cultural-historical cities sanctioned by the Chinese central government since 1994. It has several national heritage sites and dozens more provincial and prefectural ones. As a heritage city, Quzhou is not especially outstanding or unique in the vast territory of China. It is just an ordinary city of its kind and, for that matter, not much visited by cultural tourists or examined by heritage scholars apart from me and a few colleagues I have worked closely with (Hou & Wu 2012; Hou et al. 2019; Wu 2012b; Wu & Hou 2012; Zhang 2019). It is certainly less appealing than many other well-known Chinese heritage cities such as Beijing, Xi'an, Hangzhou, or Lijiang. However, the politics of heritage shaped by Western AHD and local AHDs as a fusion or interaction of the global, Chinese national, and local authoritative discourses, is no less observable in Quzhou than in other parts of China (e.g., Blumenfield & Silverman 2013; Shepherd & Yu 2013; Su & Teo 2009; Svensson & Maags 2018; Yan 2018; Zhu & Maags 2020). Postulating this in contemporary Quzhou might be an interesting project to pursue, but it is not my main concern in this Element. What I want to do, as stated earlier, is to contribute to a cultural-historical discourse approach to heritage, and particularly to rearticulating the Chinese discourse of *guji* for cultural reflections on the globalized heritage movement and its politics. In historical China, *guji* was a ubiquitous discourse, and an ordinary heritage city like Quzhou can well serve as the locality for a cultural-historical project I wish to pursue.

From a cultural-historical discourse approach, historical texts that document what we call "heritage" are of key importance. However, historical texts are usually utilized as testimony in contemporary heritage projects. In that manner, the pastness of those texts is rendered subject to the present idea of what heritage is and what values heritage has. Following Fairclough (1992), I see a text as manifestation or materialization of a discourse. Thus, a historical text about *guji* is a materialization of this particular Chinese discourse in context.

Among the most useful sources of such historical texts for studying Chinese *guji* discourse are the premodern *fangzhi* or local gazetteers. *Fangzhi* is a Chinese genre for recording a locale, as *fang* means locale, and *zhi* means documentation or written records. *Fangzhi* has been categorized as either geographic or historical writing. Some scholars view them as both historical and geographic; they are historicized geography and geographically bounded history (Yang 1999: 3). In other words, local gazetteers record historicized places and localized history. The compilation of such local gazetteers can be dated back to far ancient times in Chinese history. It is generally held that the genre came to its maturity in the Song dynasty (960–1279) and the peak of its compilation was seen in the Ming (1368–1644) and the Qing (1644–1911) eras. Most of the surviving premodern local gazetteers were compiled during this timeframe. They have been mainly used as references for governance, education, and culture- and memory-making (Cang 1990: 1–2).

Seven premodern local gazetteers of Quzhou have been found; they will serve as the data for exploring the Chinese discourse of *guji* in this Element. I should note that my distinction between "modern" and "premodern" local gazetteers is based not so much on the historical phases circumscribed by historians, but rather on the linguistic features and historical consciousness an individual local gazetteer demonstrates. The premodern local gazetteers were coded in the classical Chinese language and, more importantly, the historical consciousness that underwrote them was rooted in the Confucian historiographical tradition. In other words, the modern sense of historicity from the West had not yet exercised its considerable influence on the way they were written. These seven premodern local gazetteers of Quzhou were compiled in the late imperial and the Republican China eras, including four prefectural gazetteers and three county gazetteers. The prefectural gazetteers, bearing the same title Quzhou Prefectural Gazetteer (衢州府志), encompass local-historical records of the greater Quzhou region, which includes the present Quzhou city and some neighboring cities. My analysis, however, will concentrate primarily on the records of *guji* in the city of Quzhou.

Three of these prefectural gazetteers were compiled in the Ming dynasty. They were completed in, respectively, the sixteenth year of the Hongzhi reign (1503) by Shen Jie (沈杰), Wu Xu (吾㫤), and others, the forty-third year of the Jiajing reign (1564) by Yang Zhun (杨准), Zhao Tang (赵镗), and others, and the second year of the Tianqi reign (1622) by Lin Yinxiang (林应翔), Ye Bingjing (叶秉敬), and others. The other one was a Qing-dynasty gazetteer finished in the fiftieth year of the Kangxi reign (1710) by Yang Tingwang (杨廷望) and others.[1] The three county gazetteers are records of the Quzhou city

---

[1] The way of marking authorship of premodern Chinese local gazetteers was unique. The commissioner who compiled the local gazetteer, who was always the chief governor of the locale (county, prefecture, province), was listed first. His contribution in commissioning and sponsoring the compiling practice is called "修" (*xiu*) in Chinese. Then the chief compiler (and his major coworkers) was named. Their contribution was called "纂" (*zuan*) in Chinese. I follow the traditional order of marking authorship when I list these prefectural gazetteers and the county gazetteers later. The simplified reference to each of these gazetteers follows Zheng Yongxi's way

proper, including the two Qing-dynasty Xi'an County Gazetteers (西安县志) compiled, respectively, in the thirty-eighth year of the Kangxi reign (1699) by Chen Pengnian (陈鹏年), Xu Zhikai (徐之凯), and others, and the sixteenth year of the Jiaqing reign (1811) by Yao Baokui (姚宝煃), Fan Chongkai (范崇楷), and others, and the Qu County Gazetteer (衢县志) finished in the eighteenth year of the Republican China period (1929) by Zheng Yongxi (郑永禧, 1866–1931). For an overview of these local gazetteers, see Table 1.

The Qu County Gazetteer was not commissioned by any officials. I should note, though, that it is an excellent one, perhaps the best in quality among the seven local gazetteers (Tang 2015). The compiler, Zheng Yongxi, took five years to finish it. He eventually lost his eyesight working on the project day and night. His friend Yu Shaosong (余绍宋, 1883–1949) helped him proofread the draft and publish it (Tang 2015: 96). Zheng Yongxi was born into a family of literati and was well trained in traditional Chinese scholarship. Although the Qu County Gazetteer was compiled in the late 1920s, that is, at a time when the Chinese historiographical revolution under Western influences had spread quite widely (see Huang 1997; Wang 2001), it is regarded as a premodern local gazetteer because it is written in classical Chinese, and, as shall be seen in later sections, reflects traditional historical consciousness and ways of writing. Considering the excellence of this local gazetteer, I will not shy away from using its entries as examples in my cultural-historical discourse analysis.

Outline of Sections

This Element will present macro- and micro-analyses of the Chinese *guji* discourse in its cultural-historical contexts as an alternative to the current dominant, globalized idea of heritage. It consists of six sections. Apart from this first section, which provides an overview of the Element, and a concluding section to reflect on my findings under a philosophical lens and the insights it may shed on further research, the main body is divided into four sections.

Section 2 sets out to do a macroanalysis of the Chinese discourse of *guji* in the present and in the past. I will first explain how *guji* is defined in contemporary China, revealing its convergence with the AHD. Then I will elucidate the concept of *guji* in historical Chinese contexts through two steps: (1) an analysis of *guji* via a philological reading of the two Chinese characters that make the word, *gu* and *ji*, and (2) an analysis of the prefaces to the *guji* chapters or volumes in Chinese local

---

of referring to them. The commissioner who initiated the local gazetteer compilation was always referred to as Zheng's gazetteer.

Table 1 The seven local gazetteers of Quzhou for analysis

	Year of publication or compilation	Supervisor	Compiler(s)	Simplified reference in this volume
The Quzhou Prefectural Gazetteer	The 16th year of the Hongzhi reign, Ming dynasty (1503)	Shen Jie	Wu Xu et al.	Shen's gazetteer
–	The 43rd year of the Jiajing reign, Ming dynasty (1564)	Yang Zhun	Zhao Tang et al	Zhao's gazetteer
–	The 2nd year of the Tianqi reign (1622)	Lin Yingxiang	Ye Bingjing et al.	Ye's gazetteer
–	The 50th year of the Kangxi reign, Qing dynasty (1710)	Yang Tingwang	Yang Tingwang et al.	Yang's gazetteer
Xi'an County Gazetteer	The 38th year of the Kangxi reign (1699)	Chen Pengnian	Xu Zhikai et al.	Chen's gazetteer
–	The 16th year of the *Jiaqing* reign (1811)	Yao Baokui	Fan Chongkai et al.	Yao's gazetteer
Qu County Gazetteer	the 18th year of Republican China (1929)	–	Zheng Yongxi	Zheng's gazetteer

historiographies compiled in historical times. In so doing, I will be able to give a glimpse of the Chinese *guji* discourse compared to the mainstream notion of heritage today. It can also function as an exploration of the cultural root and context to my discourse analysis in later sections.

In the third section, I will begin a focused discourse analysis of *guji* in Quzhou in the late imperial and mid Republican eras of China, aiming to display its dynamic categorization and boundary negotiation of the past in the local past. First, I shall examine how *guji* had been categorized and recategorized in the local gazetteers of Quzhou in different ages. This reveals that there was no standardized framework to coerce the Chinese thinking of what *guji* could be. How it might be categorized was open to negotiation. In other words, the boundaries of *guji* were not fixed, but traversable. To further illustrate this understanding, I will then delineate the remembrance of natural existence, including bodies of water, trees, and stones, as *guji* in historical Quzhou, unpacking the meaning-making process through which they were transformed into culturally significant sites of memory about human figures and their deeds.

The fourth section will be devoted to the issue of materiality or physicality in Quzhou's historical discourse of *guji*. I will show that very often materiality was not a concern. When it was, the meaning-making of materiality in the *guji* discourse would be at odds with today's AHD. Most fundamentally, it was the Chinese *Li* (礼) thinking that shaped how the physical or material existence of a *guji* was meaningful. For that matter, *guji* might engender alternative cultural politics of the past. In addition, I will examine how sites, either with or without identifiable material remains, were remembered as *guji* in historical Quzhou.

Section 5 will offer a holistic view of the Chinese *guji* discourse through a focused case analysis of a particular *guji* without material remains, the House of Yin Hao. Specifically, I will conduct a cultural-historical discourse analysis of this *guji* in the local gazetteers of Quzhou. I shall demonstrate that most of the features or understandings of *guji* revealed in the previous sections, such as the neglect of materiality, meaning-making through association with historical figures and their deeds, poetry from the past as a source of meaning, and the importance of site tracing, can and usually do converge.

In the concluding section, I place my analytical findings and arguments in this Element in philosophical (and, occasionally, theological) perspectives. Reflecting on the existence of heritage in words, and the use of heritage as the use of language, I bring the cultural-historical understandings of *guji* in Quzhou to the global dialogue on what heritage is and does. It is hoped that readers will be stimulated to imagine how many different cultural words or concepts there have been in the world throughout human history.

2 *Guji* Present and *Guji* Past

> He assumed that words had kept their meaning, that desires still pointed in a single direction, and that ideas retained their logic; and he ignored the fact that the world of speech and desires has known invasions, struggles, plundering, disguises, ploys.
>
> (Foucault 1984: 76)

At the outset of his essay "Nietzsche, Genealogy, History," Foucault critiques the linear perspective underlying the German philosopher Paul Rée's history of morality, pinpointing his misconception that words, desires, and ideas are consistent or unwavering. In this section, I examine the Chinese word *guji* as a cultural concept of heritage and the ideas it has sustained. As Foucault warns, the meaning of this Chinese word and the logic of ideas it holds might not be static or constant. Presumably, it has undergone meaning transformations throughout time, especially when China began to embrace Western modernity to reshape historical consciousness and relationship with its history around the turn of the 20th century (see Huang 1997; Wang 2001). For that matter, I first look into the contemporary Chinese conceptualization of *guji* and then investigate how *guji* was understood in historical eras when the modern Western historical consciousness had not yet taken control of Chinese historical and historiographical practices.

The Contemporary Idea of *Guji*

In the contemporary Chinese context, *guji* is understood as a synonym to *wenhua yichan* (文化遗产) – the Chinese term for cultural heritage. Although in everyday interactions, *guji* is more frequently heard, these two terms may be used interchangeably in most situations. In Chinese dictionaries and encyclopedias, *guji* is usually defined as "the remains of ancient times, referring mostly to ancient architecture."[2] Baidu Encyclopedia, the Chinese counterpart to Wikipedia, equates *guji* to "*wenwu baohu danwei*" (文物保护单位), a term now officially translated as "unit of cultural heritage."[3] Let us look at how *guji* is explained in this most popular Chinese online encyclopedia:

> *Guji* (*Wenwu baohu danwei*) is historic, cultural, architectural and artistic *heritages* or *sites* left by the ancient people. It includes *ancient architecture, traditional settlements, ancient cities and streets, archeological sites, and historic and cultural remains*. It may be significant in terms of politics,

---

[2] See, for example, Xinhua Dictionary Online, http://xh.5156edu.com/html5/230525.html; and *Handian* (汉典), http://www.zdic.net/cd/ci/5/ZdicE5Zdic8FZdicA479483.htm.

[3] *Wenwu baohu danwei* refers to the immovable cultural heritage in China. It is a main part of the Chinese heritage preservation system. For more about this, see Wang (2009).

defense, religion, sacrifice, inhabitation, daily life, entertainment, labor, society, economy, education, etc. It functions to make up for the shortage of written, historic and other documentation. (My translation and emphasis)[4]

As can be seen, *guji* is clearly stated as "historic, cultural, architectural and artistic *heritages or sites*," including "*ancient architecture, traditional settlements, ancient cities and streets, archeological sites, and historic and cultural remains.*" This conceptualization of *guji* is in line with UNESCO's definition of (tangible) cultural heritage. As defined in the World Heritage Convention, "cultural heritage" includes:

> *monuments*: architectural works, works of monumental sculpture and painting, elements or structures of an archaeological nature, inscriptions, cave dwellings and combinations of features, which are of outstanding universal value from the point of view of history, art or science;
> *groups of buildings*: groups of separate or connected buildings which, because of their architecture, their homogeneity or their place in the landscape, are of outstanding universal value from the point of view of history, art or science;
> *sites*: works of man or the combined works of nature and man, and areas including archaeological sites which are of outstanding universal value from the historical, aesthetic, ethnological or anthropological point of view.
> (UNESCO 1972: 2)

In the Chinese legal framework for heritage protection, the term *wenwu* (文物) serves as the standard designation. *Wenwu* is classified into two categories: movable and immovable. Immovable *wenwu* that has been inscribed by government authorities is referred to as *wenwu baohu danwei* (文物保护单位), commonly translated as "unit of cultural heritage." This category encompasses (1) ancient *yizhi* (遗址, sites), tombs, architectural structures, cave temples, stone carvings and murals, and (2) modern historical sites, objects, and buildings associated with significant events, movements, or figures. The concept of *wenwu baohu danwei* bears a strong resemblance to contemporary ideas of *wenhua yichan* (cultural heritage) and *guji* in China.[5] This is why these terms are used interchangeably in sources such as Baidu Encyclopedia and in a variety of other public contexts.

It should be pointed out that neither *guji* nor *wenwu* in traditional China can be equated to what is now termed cultural heritage. As Wang Shu-li (2017) has

---

[4] See http://baike.baidu.com/view/112408.htm All translations hereafter are mine, if not pointed out otherwise.
[5] See Chapter 1, Article 3, in the *Law on Wenwu Protection of the People's Republic of China*. Available online at the official website of the National Cultural Heritage Administration of China: http://www.ncha.gov.cn/art/2024/11/8/art_2794_192360.html.

contended, it was under Western influence – largely through Japan as an intermediary in the early 20th century – that the concept of *wenwu* underwent a historical transformation to encompass anything of historical or aesthetic value and thus to be often used as a substitute for cultural property or cultural heritage. In far ancient China, *wenwu* was initially a term to denote significant objects in ritual systems, functioning as symbols of political power and hierarchical relations, and since the Song dynasty (960–1279) it was expanded to include various kinds of ancient objects for virtue and self-cultivation. Its modern transformation into an equivalent to cultural heritage was the result of a translingual practice (Liu 1995) that regenerates new meanings of old words through translating ostensible equivalences from the West (see also Wang & Rowlands 2017: 268–70).

This is also true to the concept of *guji*. The contemporary definition of *guji* as above outlined can be understood as a translation of or substitute by the modern discourse of cultural heritage from Europe (Li 2005). China ratified the World Heritage Convention in 1985, and the *Convention for the Safeguarding of the Intangible Cultural Heritage* in 2004. Now, the country ranks number one in both the World Heritage List and the Representative List of Intangible Cultural Heritage of Humanity, and there are numerous properties and elements on its domestic heritage lists sanctioned by the central, provincial, municipal, and county authorities. Nonetheless, the notion of heritage in contemporary China is an imported concept or, in an expression coined by the eminent 20th-century Chinese writer Lu Xun (1881–1936), "domestically made imported product" (自造的舶来品) (Lu 1973: 48). Chinese heritages are "made in China," but their "brand" and fundamental logic are global or, in most cases, Western. Professionals and researchers have translated concepts, categorizations, codes, criteria, conservation guidelines, laws, policy documents, and research publications from the developed world (Western Europe, the United States, Australia and, more recently, Japan and South Korea) and call on governmental entities and the society at large to learn from them in policy and practice (see Bi et al. 2016; Wang 2017; Zhu & Maags 2020). Adams (2013: 277) coins a phrase to speak of such a situation – "Chinese heritage management with Western characteristics." The contemporary "heritage fever" in China is a process of acquiring and implementing international knowledge and discourse.

Actually, the Chinese began to develop a modern consciousness of conserving and preserving cultural relics and ancient architecture under Western influence since the late 19th and early 20th centuries. Some scholars, such as Lai (2016) and Zhu and Maags (2020: 29–34), have traced the Chinese "journey of Westernization" in establishing their institutions, legislations and disciplinary knowledge for heritage conservation. Not only were the first Chinese public museums and legal regulations of heritage protection in the late Qing period influenced by the West, but also the academic disciplines and the professional institutions for heritage conservation in the Republican China era were established through translating or imitating Western ones, with efforts initiated by those intellectuals coming back to China with Western university degrees, notably Li Ji (李济 1896–1979) and Liang Sicheng (梁思成 1901–72) (see also Lai et al. 2004; Shepherd & Yu 2013: 9–10). Then, "much of the twentieth century saw the formation of a heritage conservation system in contemporary China, in close association with the West" (Bi et al. 2016: 198), along with the conceptual shifts, institutional developments, and discourse remaking (see Zhu & Maags 2020: chapters 2–3).

What did *guji* mean in premodern China before the Western idea of heritage influenced Chinese elites and the public? How is it divergent from the mainstream conception of heritage in contemporary China and the wider world? To provide general answers to these questions, I adopt two procedures of analysis. First, from the perspective of exegetics, I look into some ancient text fragments concerning *gu* and *ji*, so that the deeper Chinese understandings of *guji* may be unpacked. Second, I refer to the small preface (*xiaoxu*) to *guji* chapter or volume in some renowned Chinese local gazetteers. From there, expositions of what *guji* used to mean and how it was valuable can be found.

Guji as *Gu* and *Ji*

One of the most esteemed ways of explaining a word in traditional Chinese scholarship is exegetics. Adopting this approach, scholars often dismantle a multiple-character word by tracing the meaning of each of its constituent characters. In this subsection, I try to understand *guji* through explicating its two constituent characters, *gu* and *ji*.

Gu, in its literal sense, means the ancient or the past. In *Shuowen Jiezi* (说文解字), which is generally regarded as the first Chinese dictionary, Xu Shen (许慎, ca. 58 BCE–ca. 147 BCE) interprets this character as "*gu*" (故) or *raison d'être* (Xu & Duan 1981: 88). Duan Yucai (段玉裁, 1735–1815) explains, "*Raison d'être* refers to the whys and wherefores for things, which are all based on *gu* (the past). That is the reason why this interpretation—'*Gu, raison d'être*' is offered" (88). To further explicate *gu*, Duan Yucai presents two more quotations: "the heaven is *gu*; the earth is *jiu* (long-lasting)" from a most ancient Chinese historiography *Yizhoushu* (Book of Zhou), and "recollecting *gu* is in accordance with heaven" from Zheng Xuan's (郑玄, 127–200) commentaries on a pillar Chinese classic

Shangshu (Book of Documents). From these meaning expositions, it is not hard to see that *gu* had been highly valued in traditional China. The understanding of *gu* served as an essential entrée to the *raison d'être* of things in the world. *Gu* was also regarded as being connected with *Tian* (天) or Heaven – the highest being that humans on Earth should follow its way to act and live in Chinese cultural thinking (see Chan 2012; Nikkilä 1992). Recollecting *gu*, for that matter, was a way of acting in line with Heaven. It is safe to conclude that *gu* was regarded as a most crucial matter to explore for the Chinese in old times.

Another important point detected from reading the entry of *gu* in the *Shuowen Jiezi* is that *gu* was conceived of as entwined with language, particularly words from the past. As Xu Shen goes on with his explanation of the character, he states that "in terms of meaning, *gu* is composed of 'ten' (*shi*) and 'mouth' (*kou*); it means to record earlier words" (Xu & Duan 1981: 88). Duan Yucai elucidates, "It is the mouths that record earlier words. When those [words] have passed down through ten [mouths], a convention is formulated" (88). That is to say, it is through the transmission of words from the past that *gu* establishes itself.

Let us now turn to the character *ji*. As in the word *guji*, *ji* could be written as either 跡, 蹟, or 迹. Xu Shen brings them together in his dictionary. He explains the first one as "where the steps were" (70). Duan Yucai cites Zhuangzi (369 BCE – 286 BCE), an early master of Daoism, to lead us to think further, "*Ji* refers to what is produced by the shoes, but is *ji* simply about the shoes that produce them?" (70) Ostensibly, this is a rhetorical question to say that *ji* is more than the shoes that produce the footsteps. As human traces, *ji* is of fundamental value. Duan Yucai refers to the *Mao Tradition of Poetry*[6] to expose its deeper meaning, which goes, "non-observation of *ji* means deviation from the Dao" (70). This suggests that *ji* was considered to be allegorical to Dao, a primordial concept in both Daoist and Confucian thinking. Dao is extremely challenging to define, yet is often postulated as the fundamental Way by which the world exists, as well as the ultimate human pursuit (Cheng 2003).

To conclude, both *gu* and *ji* were perceived as crucial or fundamental in the Chinese tradition, relatable to and illuminating primordial Chinese concepts such as Dao and Heaven. *Gu* was considered inextricably intertwined with language and *ji* with human traces. Such a conceptualization of *guji* is more explicitly pronounced in the small prefaces (*xiaoxu*) to *guji* volumes or chapters in premodern Chinese local gazetteers.

---

[6] The *Mao Tradition of Poetry* is a commentary of the *Book of Poetry*. There were many commentaries on this Chinese classic; four have been most influential: the *Han Tradition of Poetry*, the *Qi Tradition of Poetry*, the *Lu Tradition of Poetry*, and the *Mao Tradition of Poetry*.

Understanding *Guji* in the Small Prefaces

A small preface was a common way of commencing a chapter or a volume in historiographic and other genres of writing in premodern China. As Xu Shizen (徐师曾, 1517–80) states, "A small preface is written to prelude a part or part in one's writing. To differentiate it from the big preface (*daxu*), such a name is given" (Xu 1998: 135–36). Like a big preface or, simply, preface, at the beginning of a work, a small preface is usually intended to articulate the purpose(s) of the volume, chapter, or section of one's writing. Therefore, by examining the small preface to a *guji* chapter or volume in premodern Chinese local gazetteers, I will be able to tease out the meaning and value negotiations of *guji* in historical China.

First, I will look at the small preface to the *guji* volume in the *Guangdong Provincial Gazetteer* compiled in the Yongzheng reign (1723–35) of the Qing dynasty. It reads as follows:

> Does the transmission of *gu* rely on *ji*? Or vice versa? Since the beginning of heaven and earth, [there have been] big rivers and mountains, remote rocks, and gullies. How can they not be called *gu*? But they are not *ji*. *Ji* are the traces and remains of the forerunners' tracks and ruts. That is why it is called *ji*. If so, when is not a time *ji* comes into being? There were places the renowned officials and ministers had climbed up for sightseeing, places where the literati and poets left their words, and numerous daises, pavilions, stone tablets. They were shining for a while, yet nothing would remain after they were demolished. All these are *ji*, not *gu*. Only those like the *Jiucheng* Dais, the Post of the General *Fubo*, the *Touyanchenxian* Shore, the stream called *Eyu* (crocodile), the mountain peak named *Baihe* (white crane), Across even thousands of years, those who behold them linger around in reflection, unable to depart. As for the traces of Buddhas and deities, such as the *Fuqiuzhangren*, the *Zhumingbaopu,* and the *Caoxidajian*, they, though bizarre *ji*, share the same essence of being *gu*. [古以迹传乎？抑迹以古传乎？自开辟以来，高山大川，幽岩邃壑，岂不称古？而非迹也。迹也者，前人所留之轨、所履之辙而迹遗焉，故曰迹也。顾迹亦何时蔑有？名臣巨卿之所登览，骚人词客之所留题，台榭碑铭非不林立，然而当时艳之，没即已焉，则又迹也，而非古也。惟夫九成之台，伏波之柱，投砚沉香之浦，溪记鳄鱼，峰名白鹤，千百世下，见者犹低回留之不能去。至于梵迹仙踪，若浮丘丈人、朱明抱朴、曹溪大鉴，其迹虽殊，而古则一也。][7]

Here the characters *gu* and *ji* are explained to delimit the meaning of *guji*. For the then local gazetteer compilers, *ji* referred mainly to the traces of human activity, rather than the remains of a physical structure; those that were not

---

[7] Hao Yulin 郝玉麟 et al. (supervised), Lu Zengyi 鲁曾煜 et al. (compiled). *Guangdong Provincial Gazetteer* [广东通志], *Wenyuange Complete Library in the Four Branches of Literature* version, vol. 53.

associated with human or divine beings could not be regarded as *guji*. Apparently, the globalized concept of cultural heritage and the contemporary idea of *guji* are different, as they speak primarily of the material remains inherited from the past. In the same vein, the idea of *guji* as presented in this small preface distinguishes itself from the contemporary notion of "natural heritage" that underlines the ancientness of physical or biological formations (UNESCO 1972: 3). As clearly stated, natural beings without human or divine traces could not be remembered as *guji*, no matter how far back in time they might be dated. Nonetheless, if they were known for having association with the traces of renowned human figures or divine beings, they could well be *guji*.

A further point revealed in this small preface is that *guji* was not simply about time depth or the pastness, but also about what values it might have in the present. As is known, presentness has been a key issue in both the authoritative idea of heritage and critical heritage studies. For the former, the presentness of heritage is manifested through the so-called historic, artistic, and technological values for the human race. For the latter, heritage presentness is perceived predominantly from a political point of view, as it is a site of identity, ideological, and/or rights contestations in the present (see, e.g., De Cesari 2019; Hall 1999; Harrison 2010; Littler & Nadioo 2005; Losson 2022; Smith 2004; Waterton 2010a). While critical heritage researchers treat heritage as "the root of problem" (Harvey 2024: 5) that causes contention and struggle, the Chinese hopefully saw *guji* as "a part of the solution" (5) for problems in their society and politics. Through *guji*, they should be able to excite reflections and emotions, primarily respects paid to virtuous individuals in the past. These virtuous figures would usually serve as examples or means for people to reflect on or forward critiques of pertinent problems in the present. This is more explicitly articulated in the Qing dynasty *General Gazetteer of Henan,* where the small preface to the volume of *guji* reads:

> The *junzi* (man of great virtue) in the far ancient demonstrated their virtues to benefit people, and their reputations can travel through time. They are not only recorded in the history books. The places they had stayed and visited attract later generations to pay memorial visits and linger around there reluctant to leave. Isn't that because of the personage of the *junzi*? The *Book of Poetry* remarks, "To the high hills I looked; the great way I pursued." [上古之君子，德泽加于民，名声流于时，匪独垂竹帛炳丹青而已也。其生平所经历与钧游处往往使人凭吊流连而不能去，岂非以其人哉？《诗》云: "高山仰止，景行行止。"][8]

---

[8] Tian Wenjing 田文镜, Wang Shijun 王士俊 et al. (supervised), Sun Hao 孙灏, Gu Donggao 顾栋高 et al. (compiled), *Henan Provincial Gazetteer* [河南通志], *Wenyuange Complete Library in the Four Branches of Literature* version, vol. 51. The translation of the quotation from the *Book of Poetry* is from James Legge (1876: 264).

Here, *guji* is associated particularly with *junzi* (man of great virtue) in the far past. It is their virtuous deeds and reputations that generate an aura on a *guji* and evoke emotions in visitors. With these emotions, visitors would linger around the *guji* wanting not to depart. Perceivably, these emotions or feelings were admiration and respect. This is confirmed by the ending quotation from the *Book of Poetry*. The most well-known Chinese historian Sima Qian (司马迁, ca. 145 BCE – ca. 87 BCE) also cited this when he concluded his narrative of Confucius in the *Shiji* (*Records of the Great Historian*) (Sima 1959: 1947) to show his deepest esteem to the ancient sage or *junzi* It can be said that the affective feelings toward ancient *junzi* bridges the past and the present in *guji*. As a phrase in the small preface to the *guji* chapter in the *Jiangnan General Gazetteer* (*Jiangnan Tongzhi*) goes, through *guji*, "feelings get across a hundred decades to be fused with those in the past."[9] Interestingly, a turn to emotions and affects is emerging in critical heritage studies in recent years. Scholars have shown how heritage and museum visitors' feelings and affective responses are entangled with identity politics or family attachment in heritage meaning-making (Kearney 2009; Marchant 2019; Smith 2020; Smith et al. 2018; Tolia-Kelly et al. 2017; Zhang 2020). The affectivity of *guji* in premodern Chinese contexts, as epitomized in the previous quotation, was about identification with certain individuals of virtue in history, rather than with a present community one belongs to, such as race, nation, culture, ethnicity, lineage, or family. In other words, *guji* was linked to an alternative politics based on feelings of respect and admiration toward the past, not the present recognition or inclusion of particular communities (cf. Smith 2020).

Related to such affective bonds across time directed to virtuous historical figures, *guji* was also meaningful in some other ways. For example, as the small preface to the *guji* chapter in the *General Gazetteer of Jiangnan* goes on to state, it "can also be of help to *guan* (观) and *xing* (兴)."[10] To understand this, we need to see what *guan* and *xing* mean in premodern Chinese contexts. Duan Yucai interprets *guan* by referring to *The Guliang Commentaries on the Spring and Autumn Annals*, stating, "Towards common matters, we say *shi* (视, see or watch); towards extraordinary matters, we say *guan*"(Xu & Duan 1981: 408). If this explains *guan* as a particular kind of looking or observing, the *Kangxi Dictionary*, a celebrated Chinese dictionary compiled in 1716, directs us to the deeper connotations this

---

[9] Zhao Hong'en 赵弘恩 (supervised), Huang Zhijun 黄之隽 et al. (compiled), *Jiangnan Regional Gazetteer* [江南通志], *Wenyuange Complete Library in the Four Branches of Literature* version, vol. 29.

[10] Zhao Hong'en 赵弘恩 (supervised), Huang Zhijun 黄之隽 et al. (compiled), *Jiangnan Regional Gazetteer* [江南通志], *Wenyuange Complete Library in the Four Branches of Literature* version, vol. 29.

Chinese character has. Under its entry of *guan*, one reads a quotation from the leading Song-dynasty scholar Zhu Xi's (朱熹, 1130–1200) comments on the *I Ching* (*Book of Change*) – "*Guan* means having something central and correct to show to others, and thus to be looked upon by them" (Zhang 2002: 1112). This suggests that *guan* is a value-laden act of observing and that what is exposed to *guan* should be the right and virtuous. With this understanding, it becomes clear why *guji* could assist *guan*. As pinpointed previously, *guji* was considered to be meaningful for the historical figures of virtue and later generations' affective and emotional visits aroused by their admiration and respect for those virtuous individuals in the past. In this sense, *guji* could certainly be places upon which *guan* occurs. Through the *guan* of *guji*, one would be led to the virtuous historical figures, looking upon them and learn to be a *junzi*.

Let us move to the word *xing*. In the *Commentaries on Shuowen Jiezi*, Duan Yucai remarks, "Among the six types of poetry in the *Zhouli*, there are what is called *bi* and what is called *xing*. *Xing* is to embed [our] thoughts about an event in the [poetic] speaking of things" (Xu & Duan 1981: 205). For the Chinese literati in premodern times, the connection between *guji* and poetry is intimate. On the one hand, when visiting *guji*, they often wrote poems about or for it. On the other hand, in documenting *guji* in local gazetteers, travel writing or other forms of work, poetry has an important role to play (Hou 2019; Wang 2003). By means of *xing*, the poet can lead people to more profound meanings and concerns. The Qing Chinese scholar Yao Chenxu's (姚承绪) *Wuyue Fanggu Lu* (吴越访古录 *Records of Visiting the Past in the Wu and Yue regions*) well epitomizes this. In that work, which intends to document *guji* in Wu and Yue (roughly, Zhejiang, Jiangsu, and Shanghai today), he amassed 546 poems of his own for the task. Cheng Tingwu (程庭鹭), a friend of the author, exposes in the preface to the book the deep meaning underlying such poetic writing of *guji*:

> Places are to render known human beings, and human beings are to render known places. [This volume] demonstrates the author's capacity in reading humans and expounding the world. It brings to light what is obscure and makes manifest what is minute, not simply a work to show off poetic talent. (Cheng 1999: 1)

In this perspective, *guji* can be places that endorse the full play of *xing*. When reading a poem about a *guji*, one appreciates not only the poet's literary talent but also the profound and delicate meanings beneath the poetic lines to understand the past and the present human world. Through such poetic writings or *xing*, both the *guji* it describes and the historic figures it commemorates get passed down to later generations.

To synthesize the insights gained in this macroanalysis of *guji*, I reiterate four main divergences between this repressed Chinese concept and the mainstream conceptualization of heritage today:

(1) *Guji* is predominantly about human and, sometimes, divine beings. It is their deeds and virtues that render *guji* meaningful and appealing to people. As such, it differentiates from the universalized notion of (tangible) cultural heritage, which rests heavily on the material remains of the past and the so-called innate values within its materiality or physicality.

(2) *Guji* does not include pure natural creations. What is called "natural heritage" today could not be remembered as *guji* in traditional Chinese contexts. However, this is not to mean that the natural beings could not be *guji*. A stream or a mountain peak might fall into the category of *guji* if they have traces of memorable human or divine beings.

(3) *Guji* is not simply a matter of the past; presentness is its overriding concern. Different from our concern over the presentness of heritage as a site of political control and contestation, *guji* is deemed to be a resource for critiquing or rethinking the present through value-laden acts of *guan* (looking or observing) to learn from the right and the correct, as well as the affective bondage it establishes with historical figures of virtue.

(4) *Guji* is also linked to language, especially poetic language that embodies *xing* to negotiate delicate and profound meanings concerning the present. This is still neglected in contemporary heritage practices, though critical heritage researchers have problematized the language of present experts and policy texts.

In the ensuing sections, I will present cultural-historical discourse analysis of *guji* recorded in Quzhou local gazetteers to demonstrate how the Chinese represented, constructed, and made meaning of the past within this forgotten cultural discourse of heritage. With different focuses, they serve as a crystallization of the fundamental logic of ideas associated with *guji*.

3 What Can *Guji* Be? The Categorization and Boundary Negotiation of *Guji*

> [A]s I read the passage, all the familiar landmarks of my thought – our thought, the thought that bears the stamp of our age and our geography – breaking up all the ordered surfaces and all the planes with which we are accustomed to tame the wild profusion of existing things, and continuing long afterwards to disturb and threaten with collapse our age-old distinction between the Same and the Other.
>
> (Foucault 1989: xvi)

As Foucault has shown in many of his works (1972, 1977, 1989), debunking the categorization or order of things under a notion can be an expedient means to unravel knowledge production and modes of thinking. It is a fertile approach to studying how a concept or an object is discursively constructed to shape the ways we think and act. In this section, I explicate the categorization of *guji* in Quzhou from late imperial to mid Republican periods (specifically, 1500s–1920s). By examining how *guji* is categorized, including how natural beings, such as trees and stones, could be classified into its realm, I will show, from a particular angle, alternative ways of constructing the past in a specific local-historical context, and thereby stimulate reflections on contemporary heritage research and practice that usually presuppose a system of categorization endorsed by international authoritative organizations, such as UNESCO and International Council on Monuments and Sites (ICOMOS).

Categorizing and Recategorizing *Guji*

In Quzhou, before the modern Western ideas of history and historic conservation had become decisively influential, what could (not) be said in the discourse of *guji*? How did *guji* as a discourse order or classify things in Quzhou from late imperial to mid Republican eras of China? With these questions in mind, I have analyzed the seven premodern local gazetteers from a cultural-historical discourse perspective. Those questions are then transformed into some more specific ones: In the examined local gazetteers, what is included in the category of *guji*? What subcategories of *guji* can be found? What upper category could *guji* be assigned to? And what categories ran parallel to it? In this section, I report my findings regarding these specific questions from examining the seven local gazetteers of Quzhou one by one. Then I conclude with a discussion on what such historical modes of categorization tell us about the forgotten Chinese idea of *guji*, particularly in terms of boundary thinking.

In Shen's gazetteer, *guji* constitutes a section or category in its seventh volume, which does not have a title (other volumes in the gazetteer are without titles too). Along with *guji*, the only other section in the volume is *siguan* (寺观, Temples and Monasteries). That is to say, the compilers of Shen's gazetteer considered *guji* a parallel category to that of temples and monasteries, and a higher-level category that can accommodate these two might be difficult, if not impossible, to assign. Furthermore, it is found that *guji* is further classified geographically in Shen's gazetteer. Specifically, different *guji* show themselves under such titles as *Fu* (府), *Xi'an* (西安), *Longyou* (龙游), *Jiangshan* (江山), *Changshan* (常山), and *Kaihua* (开化), which were then counties under the administration of the Quzhou prefecture. This is a common way through which a prefectural gazetteer organizes its records under a category undividable otherwise. Therefore, we can say that the compilers of Shen's gazetteer did not consider *guji* as having subtypes, or worthwhile to be classified into subtypes.

In Zhao's gazetteer, the category of *guji* is seen in the third volume, *Shanchuanji Er* (山川纪二, The Record of Mountains and Rivers II), with such parallel categories as *Jindu* (津渡, Ferries), *Piyan* (陂堰, Lakes and Weirs), and *Tangjin* (塘井, Pools and Wells). In the section on *guji*, one finds almost the same geographical subclassification as seen in Shen's gazetteer. This, again, means *guji* was not able or worthwhile to be further divided into subtypes for the compilers of Zhao's gazetteer.

A somewhat different picture unfolds in Ye's gazetteer. In the volume *Yudi Zhi* (*Geographic Records*), records of *guji* constitute an individual chapter, along with parallel chapters such as *Xingye* (星野, Hoshino), *Shengzhai* (圣宅, The House of the Sage's Descendants), *Jiangyu* (疆域, Territory), *Yange* (沿革, Historic Transitions), *Xingsheng* (形胜, Landscapes), *Fangxiang* (坊乡, Urban Neighborhoods and the Countryside), and *Yandu* (堰渡, Weirs and Ferries). Although under the chapter of *guji* is, again, a geographical subclassification, as seen in the two earlier Quzhou gazetteers mentioned, in the table of contents of Ye's gazetteer, ten subtypes are named under the category of *guji*: *Cheng* (城, Cities), *Zhai* (宅, Houses/Mansions), *Lou* (楼, Towers), *Ge* (阁, Pavilions), *Ting* (亭, Kiosks), *Tai* (台, Daises), *Tang* (堂, Halls), *Miao* (庙, Temples), *Ci* (祠, Memorial Temples), and *Mu* (墓, Tombs) (Lin et al. 2009: 365). This means that for the compilers of Ye's gazetteer, *guji* could be further classified into these different subcategories.

Surprisingly, no specific volume, chapter, or section on *guji* is identified in Yang's gazetteer. However, this does not mean that what is recorded under the category of *guji* in the earlier local gazetteers of Quzhou is excluded from this local gazetteer. Rather, they are scattered in several different volumes of it, such as *Shanchuan* (山川, Mountains and Rivers), *Xieyu* (廨宇, Government Buildings), *Fangxiang* (坊巷, Neighborhoods and Alleys), and more. Thus, it is fair to say that, in Yang's gazetteer, *guji* as a category is buried or dissolved.

In Chen's gazetteer, a chapter on *guji* is located in the volume of *Shanchuan*, along with parallel chapters *Zhi Shan* (志山 Recording Mountains), *Zhi Dongyan* (志洞岩, Recording Caves and Rocks), *Zhi Chuan* (志川, Recording Rivers), *Wuchan* (物产, Natural and Agricultural Products). In the chapter of *guji*, there are no further subcategories given.

Finally, in Yao's gazetteer and Zheng's gazetteer' *guji* has the privilege of constituting an independent volume. While the former does not encompass any subcategories of *guji*, six of them are found in the latter gazetteer. They are, in sequence: (1) *Gucheng* (故城, Ancient Cities), (2) *Jiushu* (旧署, Old Official Seats), (3) *Fangxiang* (坊巷, Blocks and Alleys), (4) *Ta* (塔, Pagodas), (5) *Zhaidi Yuanting* (宅第园亭, Mansions, Gardens and Pavilions), with *Loutai Chitang* (楼台池塘, Towers, Daises, Ponds, and Pools) supplemented, and (6) *Zhongmu* (冢墓, Tombs).

From these findings, it becomes clear that the classification of *guji* was not static or rigid in Quzhou from the 1500s to the 1920s. To which upper category *guji* should belong and how it could be divided into subcategories was rather elastic. With the vicissitudes of time, local gazetteer compilers might have varying understandings or considerations about their *guji* documentation and thus chose to order it in quite different manners. In other words, how *guji* should be classified or ordered was open to negotiation for the premodern local gazetteer compilers. There was no standard for them to follow. As such, it contrasts with UNESCO's World Heritage framework, as well as the national and local heritage frameworks in different countries forged with direct or indirect influence from the World Heritage framework. Today, in China and the wider world, heritage is commonly perceived as a system that consists of cultural heritage, natural heritage, and cultural landscape. Other categories would be extremely hard, if not impossible, to get in. Furthermore, each of these subcategories of heritage is clearly defined to exclude one another. They are further separated into definable subtypes, and those subtypes are classifiable as well. For example, we divide cultural heritage into tangible and intangible cultural heritage, and tangible heritage into monuments, sites, and groups of buildings. Such a systematic categorization of heritage has been taken for granted in practices and most of our research. It serves as basic or fundamental knowledge that coerces our thinking of and actions upon heritage. In recent critical heritage studies, the nature–culture divide in this system of heritage conceptualization continues to be criticized, even though the category of cultural landscape was added into UNESCO's world heritage framework in 1992. The deep root of this problem, as critical researchers have pointed out, is the Western dualist thinking that separates a wholeness into two binary parts (see, e.g., Brown, 2023; Harrison 2015; Katelieva et al. 2020).

With this analysis of *guji* categorization and recategorization in historical Quzhou, what I can add is that the system of heritage is problematic in that it sets up clear-cut boundaries and discards relational, dynamic, and transformative thinking. In the Chinese cultural context, dual categorizations are common. A fundamental one is the *yin–yang* thinking, which orders the world and matters therein into two categories, *yin* and *yang*. However, *yin* and *yang* are not separable, definite categories that exclude one another; they are rather dynamic and relative. *Yin and yang* are "experienced as a matter of degrees of contrast," and they are divided "based on our limited experience and special ends from our understanding of *yin* and *yang* as cosmic forces and states of becoming" (Cheng 2008: 75; see also Graham 1986). Furthermore, "*yin* and *yang* are related in many intimate, reciprocal and interactive ways: *yang* can be said to bring out *yin*, just as *yin* can be said to bring out *yang*"; they are "mutually supporting, transforming, balancing, enhancing and furthering of the new" (Cheng 2008: 75; see also Fang 2012). The boundary between *yin* and *yang* is open and changeable. In the same vein, the boundaries of *guji* are also dynamic and open to negotiation. It could be categorized and recategorized differently throughout time.

I should note that I am not suggesting a complete absence of convergence in the ways how *guji* was classified across time. As described earlier, some similar subtypes of *guji* are seen in Ye's gazetteer and Zheng's gazetteer. What I hope to contend is that the then local gazetteer compilers had the privilege to express different understandings in compartmentalizing *guji*, without a standardized system of classification to coerce their thinking. Through designing their categorizations of *guji* with a similar basic idea of what it could and could not be, the local gazetteer compilers might extend intellectual dialogue with those doing parallel projects in the past and in the future. This is clearly articulated in the section of *Fanli* (凡例, Principles of compilation) of Chen's gazetteer:

> The ways of naming and grouping are generally similar in different prefectural and county gazetteers. Divergences and distinctions occur mainly due to diverse understandings. They are not deliberately made to look different.[11]

A more elaborate expression of this is found in the *Fanli* section of Zheng's gazetteer:

> Chen's gazetteer places *guji* in the volume of Mountains and Rivers, which might make it oversimplistic. Yao's gazetteer has recorded more [*guji*]. I have collected even more and attempted to trace the provenances and transformations they have gone through. Therefore, I give *guji* an individual volume, so as to satisfy the desire of later generations for studying the past. (Zheng 1984: 5)

Here, Zheng Yongxi extends dialogue with earlier local gazetteer compilers, arguing that *guji* should not simply be a subcategory of *Shanchuan*, but needs to be an ultimate rubric to include more. His treatment of *guji* as a category was based on what he had found in his research, as well as his understanding of later generations' expectation of *guji* as a resource for studying the past or, rather, his

---

[11] Chen Pengnian 陈鹏年 (supervised), Xu Zhikai 徐之凯 et al. (compiled), (1699). *Xi'an County Gazetteer* [西安县志], Kangxi 38th year version, the introductory volume.

own expectation of *guji* as such a resource for later generations. In this manner, his dialogue on (the writing of) *guji* is directed to both previous- and later-generation colleagues and those interested in studying the past.

Ultimately, it can be said that the categorization of *guji* was more about boundary negotiation than boundary setting for the Chinese in historical times, which was in line with their *yin–yang* thinking. Though working to delimit what *guji* could be and how they could be ordered, it was contingent, dynamic, and open to dialogue. Such a dialogical and dynamic boundary thinking was not only reflected in the making and remaking of *guji* categorization, but also in the transformation of non-*guji* into *guji*, such as the remembering of natural beings as *guji*.

Natural Beings as *Guji*

As observed in Section 2, *guji* does not include what is today categorized as natural heritage, but natural beings might be recognized as *guji* if they could be linked to human or divine figures. From the *yin–yang* perspective, one can say this is a manifestation of the Chinese understanding of nature and culture as relative, interactive, and transformative binaries, and of *guji* as having unsettled, negotiable boundaries. Through examination of the seven local gazetteers of Quzhou, I have identified several instances of natural beings recorded as *guji*. These include specific bodies of waters, trees, and stones. Table 2 catalogs the documented natural elements as *guji* in the local gazetteers under scrutiny.

As displayed in Table 2, natural beings as *guji* were an evolving idea over time. In Shen's gazetteer, no natural beings were recognized as *guji*. In Zhao's and Ye's gazetteers, only bodies of water could be remembered as *guji*. Then stones became *guji* in Chen's gazetteer. In Yao's and Zheng's gazetteers, trees were added in the rubric. Among the three types of natural beings, bodies of water seem to be more readily recognizable as *guji*. This might be because they were more often associated with historical events, human figures, and their poetic writings than stones and trees were. As the boundaries of *guji* were not static but open to negotiation, trees and stones could be recognized by this Chinese discourse of "heritage" and recorded for remembrance. It should also be observed that, though the transmission of *guji* was mostly constant across time, a particular natural being recognized and recorded as *guji* in one local gazetteer might not always be recognized in another. One can find more or less variations in the documentation of natural beings as *guji* across the seven inspected local gazetteers of Quzhou. This, again, confirms that there was no standardized idea or uniform definition of *guji*.

To further explicate such dynamic conceptualization and boundary negotiations of *guji*, I now turn to examine a few records of trees and stones as found in the *guji*

Table 2 Natural beings as *guji* in the seven local gazetteers of Quzhou

Shen's gazetteer	None
Zhao's gazetteer	The Bailian Pond (白莲池), the Ling Pond (菱塘), Sir Yang's River (杨公河)[12]
Ye's gazetteer	Sir Yang's River
Yang's gazetteer	No *guji* section/chapter/volume
Chen's gazetteer	The Small Emei Peak (小峨眉峰),[13] the Bailian Pond (白莲池), the Ling Pond
Yao's gazetteer	The Bailian Pond, the Small Emei Peak, the Zhanlong Pines (战龙松), the Five-Finger Camphor (五枝樟), the Ancient Camphor (古樟树)
Zheng's gazetteer	The Bailian Pond, the Small Emei Peak, the Baishou Stone (百寿石), the Zhanlong Pines, the Five-Finger Camphor, the Ancient Camphor

part of Quzhou's seven local gazetteers. These two types of natural beings are chosen as they are less likely to be considered as heritage today. To delve into these records can better illustrate the boundary-crossing nature of *guji*-making.

Trees as Guji

As is known, cultural landscape was added to the World Heritage Convention in 1992 to recognize the combined works of nature and human beings, in response to the critiques against the "nature–culture" dichotomy in Western-originated heritage thinking. However, in this more inclusive heritage framework, can trees or stones be considered heritage? The answer may still be negative. At least, one does not find any trees or stones in the World Heritage List. In the Registration Forms for the Third National Survey of Immovable Heritage (Quzhou) in 2009, no documentation of trees or stones can be identified either. Nonetheless, for people in China and many other parts of the world, trees might be important places of historic significance or sites of memory. For instance, in Kaiija, northwestern Tanzania, there is a huge tree shrine near a village that functions as a compelling mnemonic for the ancient history of Kaiija, and the focal point of identity for social groups such as the royal clan and the Indigenous ironworking clan (Schmidt 2010). And a few miles north of Cibecue in Western Apache, locals may point one to a huge

---

[12] The Ling Pond and Sir Yang's River were merged in one, as we read in the record of the Ling Pond, "[located on] the left side behind the Cha Court in the eastern city, that is now the Sir Yang's River" (Zhao Tang et al. 2009: 164; Yao Baokui et al. 1970: 533; Zheng Yongxi 1984: 776). That might explain why most local gazetteers does not include Sir Yang's River.

[13] The Small Emei Peak (小峨眉峰) is actually two stones, see later for the record and analysis.

cottonwood tree at Gizhyaa'itiné (Trail Goes Down between Two Hills). Amusing stories about Old Man Owl and two beautiful sisters who tried to tease the senior amorist with open legs standing in the tree have been told from generation to generation, shaping Apache people's morality and sense of place (see Basso 1996: 61–5). In early 20th-century Sweden, "a great and beautiful juniper," "a giant spruce," "a 'troll' pine," and "a majestic old oak" were recorded as *naturminnesmärker*, a concept that means "a combination of nature, remembrance, and mark (trace)" (Sundin 2005: 13). Are these trees heritage? If yes, what kind of heritage are they: natural, cultural, or cultural landscape heritage? For me, they do not seem to be straightforwardly categorizable into the contemporary idea of heritage. Elsewhere, I have examined how in the discourse of *guji* trees were remembered in Qing-dynasty Hangzhou, the capital city of Zhejiang province. I have argued that tree *guji* might be more analogous to cultural or cultural landscape heritage, yet still with observable cultural distinctiveness of its own (Hou 2019). Here, my examination of trees as *guji* in the historical context of Quzhou is quite similar, but more focused on individual cases. My aim here is to illustrate the dynamics of boundary negotiation, rather than the more general apparatus of meaning-making in the Chinese cultural discourse of *guji*.

As shown in Table 2, three tree *guji* were recognized in Qing and Republican Quzhou, namely, the Zhanlong Pines (战龙松), the Five-Finger Camphor (五枝樟), and the Ancient Camphor (古樟树). My case analysis will be based on the documentation of the first two, through which I hope to further challenge the globalized, standardized framework of heritage categorization and, more importantly, showcase Chinese cultural-historical understanding of boundary negotiation in ordering the past in the local past. The first one is the Zhanlong Pines, a group of pine trees on a famous mountain of Quzhou. In Yao's gazetteer the record of it reads as follows:

> Example 1–1
> **The Zhanlong Pines** Located in the Keshan Mountain. It has been told that there used to be a stone tablet with three characters – *Zhan Long Song* – carved on it. The characters were Zhu Huian's calligraphy. The broken pieces of the stone tablet were still identifiable during the Qianlong reign (1736–95). Now they are lost. (Zhou Zhao's poem) The green characters have gone from the Zhanlong trees, the red pavilion having retreated in the Luming Mountain.
>
> [**战龙松** 在柯山,相传有朱晦庵书战龙松三字碑,乾隆间犹存断碣,今失去。(周召诗) 绿字已销战龙松,红亭空隐鹿鸣山。] (Yao et al. 1970: 569)

Noticeably, this documentation of the Zhanlong Pines shows little concern over the trees as natural entities. Or, in other words, these pine trees as natural beings were not considered important for their meaning-making as a local *guji*. The attention of the gazetteer compilers at the time was on some cultural and historical matters related to these pine trees, including (1) the stone tablet that names these pines and (2) the calligraphy of Zhu Huian, better known as Zhu Xi (朱熹, 1130—1200), that renders this stone tablet and these pine trees special and valuable. As such, these pines were called into being in the human world: They were named, remembered (as the act of erecting a stone tablet with its name beside them is a mnemonic practice), and liaised with Zhu Xi, a most influential Confucian scholar in the Chinese intellectual history, who had been worshiped as an accompanying deity in the sacrifice to Confucius in late imperial China (see, for example, Zhao et al. 1976: 2533). It was this distinguished and venerated historical figure and his calligraphy that rendered these pine trees significant and worthwhile to remember, even though the stone tablet that could attest to this cultural significance had already disappeared at the time it was documented. Indeed, a group of pines by themselves could not make a *guji*. Only through entering into the human world to break the boundary between nature and culture might they become a memorable *guji*. What is more, this boundary-breaking process ought to be based on the natural being's cultural association with a memorable historic figure and words – in this case, Zhu Xi's handwritten characters to name these pines.

In addition, one sees two lines of a poem cited to document the pine trees as *guji*. Reproducing these poetic lines in which the Zhanlong Pines were referred to, the local gazetteer compilers made meaning of the pines via the poetic words of Zhou Zhao. This is a further means to call the pine trees into being in the world of humans. As Tuan Yi-fu (1991: 691) has pointed out:

> The Chinese characteristically believe that poems and poetic prose can deepen meanings of landscape. They have not actually said that words call objects into being, wake up rocks and flowers, imbuing them with life and meaning, and yet something of that belief is there.

Thus, these pines would transcend the boundaries between nature and culture and demonstrate their quality as a *guji* to incite *xing*. Meanwhile, this renders the well-known local scholar Zhou Zhao, whose name and biography are seen in the local gazetteer's volume dedicated to Confucian scholars (see Yao et al. 1970: 1295–96), pertinent to these pine trees. As such, the pines are further incorporated into the realm of *guji*. As pointed out earlier, this Chinese idea of heritage is more about human traces than about the physical vestiges; its meanings and values are derived chiefly from the historical figures associated with it.

In Zheng's gazetteer, the record of the Zhanlong Pines appears to be rather multifarious. Its main body reads:

> Example 1–2
>
> (The Kangxi County Gazetteer) In front of the Shiqiao Temple in the Keshan Mountain is a sequestered track. Several pines grow there. They are all over a thousand years old and are called the Zhanlong Pines. (*Wuzazu* by Xie Zhaozhi in the Ming dynasty) In the Lankeshan Mountain of Sanqu,[14] there are several pines huddling up together. They appear alien and enigmatic. I once passed by and signed for their being in such a bleak place, unable to attract viewers. Beside the track are a dozen stone tablets of tribute, reading "*Zhan Long Song*" (Zhanlong Pines). The characters were Zhu Huiweng's calligraphy.
>
> [(康熙县志) 柯山石桥寺寺门前山径幽寂, 有虬松数株, 皆千余年物, 名战龙松。(明谢肇淛五杂俎) 三衢烂柯山中有数松盘挐蹙缩, 形势殊诡, 余尝过之叹其生于荒僻, 无能赏者。又十数武石碣表于道周, 大书曰: "战龙松", 朱晦翁笔之。] (Zheng 1984: 784)

Here, the location, natural setting and physical appearance of the pine trees are accounted for. This might indicate that the existence of these pine trees in the natural world is also meaningful in the *guji* making of them. It is important to reiterate, however, that in traditional Chinese contexts, *guji* does not encompass purely natural beings in isolation. The description of these pines in their natural settings, I contend, appears to be a subjective documentation of them as a *jing* (景, landscape), since one can easily detect a human view of them. For the Chinese, *jing* "is highly subjective, and [it] borrows its charm from human thoughts and sentiments" (Lin 1937: 437). As I have illustrated elsewhere, in Qing-dynasty Hangzhou, trees could be remembered as *guji* if they were considered most beautiful or rare *jing* (Hou 2019: 458–59). Likewise, the *Zhonglong* Pines were recognized as a *guji* as they, first of all, constituted a rare *jing* to be viewed. As displayed in the Ming dynasty scholar–official Xie Zhaozhi's (谢肇淛, 1567–1624) words cited, the pines were to him a *jing* rare, bizarre and sentiment provoking – Xie Zhaozhi signed for their being in such a bleak place. In the eminent Chinese landscape scholar Xie Ninggao's term, these pine trees can incite the "human-landscape effect," that is, "the inspiration, evocation, edification, sensation, empathy, engagement or any other possible spiritual or psychological responses from humans when facing a *jing*" (Xie 1991: 19). In addition, through citing Xie Zhaozhi's work, the local gazetteer complier further rendered the pines into a human *ji* not only of Zhu

---

[14] *Sanqu* is another name for Quzhou.

Xi, but also of Xie Zhaozhi himself. As a famous official, writer, and traveler, Xie was recognized and recorded in the *History of Ming* (see Zhang et al. 1974: 7357). This historical figure "once passed by and signed for" these pines also contributed to bringing them to the cultural sphere.

Finally, this documentation of the Zhanlong Pines as *guji* ends with more quotations in smaller-sized characters: poetic lines of Ye Nansheng (叶南生) in the Ming dynasty and Ye Rizhen (叶日蓁) in the Qing dynasty (Zheng 1984: 784). This way, the Zhanlong Pines were further associated with locally significant poets in history, whose virtues were recognized in Quzhou local histories (see, e.g., Zheng 1984: 2304, 2372). In the meantime, these poems contribute to rendering the pine trees a site of poetics (Hou 2019: 460–61) or a landscape for poetic *xing*, and thereby a *guji* worthwhile to remember.

Stones as Guji

As listed in Table 2, two entries of stone *guji* are found in the local gazetteers of Quzhou under analysis: the Baishou Stone (百寿石) and the Small Emei Peak (小峨眉峰), which refers actually to two stones. Here I look at the record of the Small Emei Peak to demonstrate how stones might enter into the realm of *guji*.

> Example 2–1
> **The Small Emei Peak** (*Records of Places of Interest*) [It is] in front of the seat of the prefectural government [of Quzhou]. During the *Qianfu* reign (874–79) of the Tang dynasty, the prefect Ji Gou got two stones when establishing a stockade at the Dragon Mountain. They were over six *chi*[15] long. He had it placed at the *Wenhui* Pavilion. During the *Chunhua* reign (990–94) of the Song dynasty, the prefect Shen Zhili relocated the stones here and covered them up with earth to form a peak. Later generations had taken them as the tomb of Guo Pu (276–324). During the *Shaosheng* reign (1094–98), the prefect Sun Ben dug up the stones and moved them to the hall of the prefectural government. Later, in the *Xuanhe* reign (1119–25), the prefect Gao Zhilin placed them back. It was said that the seat of the prefectural government was at a position suppressed by Mount Emei, the stones were placed here to resist that, and they were called "Small Emei." The prefect Li Sui (1504–66) in the Ming dynasty dug out the two stones again, and relocated them beside the Youzhu Pavilion, with an inscriptional record written for them.
>
> [小峨眉峰 (名胜志) 在郡治前。唐乾符间刺史季觏置砦龙山, 得石长六尺许, 取置文会阁。宋淳化间郡守慎知礼移植于此, 积土为峰。后遂讹传为郭璞墓。绍圣中郡守孙贲发之, 因徙此石, 移置堂中。宣和间郡守高至临复移归故处。相传为峨眉山正压郡治, 故处此以对之, 因名"小峨眉"。明郡守李遂又发去双石, 植游瞩亭之侧, 有记。] (Yao et al. 1970: 567–68; Zheng 1984: 780)

---
[15] *Chi* is a traditional Chinese unit of length. One *chi* approximately equals to or slightly longer than one foot.

This entry of the Small Emei Peak presents a chain of stories concerning the two stones, narrating how they were found and were dealt with in the passage of time. In this way, the stones are associated with a number of historical figures significant in the local past. These include five prefects of Quzhou: Ji Gou in the Tang dynasty, Shen Zhili, Sun Ben and Gao Zhilin in the Song dynasty, and Li Sui in the Ming dynasty. Also pertinent is a prominent scholar–official in the Jin dynasty, namely, Guo Pu. Albeit a mistaken association, it adds an enigmatic zest to the stones as a *guji*, making them more culturally enthralling. As stated earlier, it is these associations with historical figures that make the stones culturally meaningful and thereby acceptable as a *guji*.

From another point of view, this record of the stones presents a "cultural biography of objects" (Gosden & Marshall 1999) or "material biography" (Meskell 2021) of them. As Gosden and Marshall (1999: 170) state, "Not only do objects change through their existence, but they often have the capability of accumulating histories, so that the present significance of an object derives from the persons and events to which it is connected." As narrated, the stones had been accumulating history throughout time, from the Tang dynasty to the Ming dynasty, and making connections to the historical figures and their deeds as prefects in Quzhou. In such a biography, the stones, which were originally objects from the natural world, were imbued with cultural and historical meanings. Thus, they could serve as a *guji* for remembrance, or a site of memory "to block the work of forgetting" (Nora 1989: 19).

In this entry of the Small Emei Peak as *guji*, there is also an annotation after its main body just analyzed. In that annotation, we read stories related to the stones with more details. For example, Sun Ben' digging up the stones is narrated as follows.

> Example 2–2
> Beside Quzhou's prefectural government hall, a hump used to be seen. It was said the hump was an ancient tomb. There, on a stone tablet, was written, "The prefects shall be my cemetery men for five hundred years." This had been passed down from generation to generation. No one dared to slight it. In the first year of the Shaosheng reign (1094), Sun Ben from Qi'an was the prefect. He asked his men about the hump and was told the said story. He ordered it to be demolished. Local officials were terrified. Sun Ben said, "Even if there're bones of the ancient man of virtue under that hump, we should relocate them in line with the ritual laws." He then wrote a eulogy and offered sacrifices by himself. He demolished the hump and dug further into the earth for several meters.[16] Nothing special was found except two stones . . .

---

[16] *Zhang* (丈) is a Chinese measurement. One *zhang* is about 3.33 meters. ☐ is used to refer to a character unrecognizable in the original. One may guess that the word is 许 or 余. Not knowing that character exactly, I suppose it is safe to translate "丈☐" into several meters.

[衢州厅事下旧有土势隆起，相传云古坟冢也。旧有碑云："五百年刺史为吾守墓。"以此前后相承，皆畏而不敢慢。绍圣元年，齐安孙公贲为守，问之左右，以是对公。命毁之，官吏大恐。公曰："藉令土有贤者骨，当以礼法迁之。"乃为文，自祭而除之。劚深丈□，了无他异，但有二石......] (Yao et al. 1970: 568; see also Zheng 1984: 780)

This is a more complete narrative about how Sun Ben demolished the hump and excavated out the two stones. Reading this, one can envision this historical figure's brave character as a local governor of virtue. Such virtuous historical figures and their deeds, as mentioned in Section 2, are of crucial significance in making the stones a unique *guji* to remember.

Finally, it should be noted that the contexts in which the two stones were placed are also important. As Godden and Marshall (1999: 174) contend, contexts can "create meanings and produce object biographies." Easily inferable from the above narrative, the stones were assigned diverse meanings when they were arranged at different places. A particularly interesting instance is that the two stones were relocated in front of the prefectural government of Quzhou as a strategy to resist the suppression from Mount Emei and, thus, were called Small Emei. As Mount Emei, a renowned mountain in southwestern China, is over a thousand miles away from Quzhou, the suppressing effect it might have upon the prefectural government was only conceivable from the perspective of *feng shui* (风水), which, as Zhang Su (2018) demonstrates, is still influential in Chinese heritage narratives and practices today. In other words, the two stones were attached a *feng shui* meaning when they were relocated beside the prefectural government.

To conclude this section, here are the beginning sentences of the small preface to *guji* in Chen's gazetteer:

> When a person, amidst the dust or tangled wilderness, comes across a fist-sized stone, a handful of water, a cupful of soil, or a wood of ten feet long, they cannot help but linger, sighing with emotion, their heart pounding uncontrollably. Why is this so? It is because there is someone who has tied with them! Those who are so much held in esteem must surely possess aspirations and ideals within themselves, manifested in their significance through great accomplishments in their times. How, then, could their value be confined to such trifling things as springs, stones, soil, or wood?
>
> [凡人于埃塿灌莽中得一拳石，一掬水，一杯之土，寻丈之木，辄从而流连慨想怦怦焉不能自已者，何也? 有人焉以系之也! 夫人之足以见重者，必自有其抱负于身，表见于当世之具，而岂系此区区泉石土木之间哉?][17]

---

[17] Chen Pengnian 陈鹏年 (supervised), Xu Zhikai 徐之凯 et al. (compiled), (1699). *Xi'an County Gazetteer* [西安县志], Kangxi 38th year version, vol. 3.

Indeed, the suppressed Chinese idea of *guji* does not value or respect things in the natural world themselves, but the human figures of virtue and their deeds associated with those things. Historically, the Chinese have not developed a rigid categorization of *guji*, or a universally applicable framework to assess what can(not) be categorized into the rubric because even those plain things in the wilderness, such as a stone, a spring, some soil, or a piece of wood might be regarded as *guji*, not to mention those cultural places, historic buildings, or religious sites. This is rather similar to Nora's (1989) idea of *lieux de mémoire* or site of memory. As one might have noticed, Nora and his followers often offer a set of instances to exemplify different types of them for their purposes of exposition. They do not have a rigid categorization of *lieux de mémoire*. For both these ideas, categorization and recategorization are only contingent ways of delimiting. They are situated in and open to dialogue with others in the past and in the future.

That said, I can ask a few challenging questions concerning today's heritage research and practice: Should the World Heritage system and its way of heritage categorization be rigidly followed in China and other parts of the world? Or should we set up a rigid system to compartmentalize various heritages worldwide? How should we perceive and deal with Chinese *guji* or whatever cultural concepts that cannot be readily put into the globalized catalogue of heritage? Inspired by the dynamic and dialogical ways of categorizing *guji*, I argue that heritage does not need to be defined and classified so unbendingly. There is no one best categorization of heritage that all should follow. The globalized system of heritage categories sets up boundaries and distinctions between heritage and nonheritage, as well as among different subtypes of heritage, which should not simply be problematized and remedied but deconstructed as a whole. This is not to suggest that all those familiar subcategories of heritage are no longer valid. They still are. Only the system they constitute should no longer be a universal model to follow. Taking such a system as universally applicable only makes heritage standardized, static and homogenous, which is at odds with the fundamental objective of the World Heritage program, that is, to preserve and promote cultural diversity.

4 The Materiality/Physicality of *Guji*

[T]he paradox is that the very past which seems to penetrate everything, and to manifest itself with such surprising vigour, is also strangely evading our physical grasp. This same China, which is loaded with so much history and so many memories, is also oddly deprived of ancient monuments. In the Chinese landscape, there is a material absence of the past that can be most disconcerting for cultivated Western travellers – especially if they approach China with the criteria and standards that are naturally developed in a European environment.

(Ryckmans 1986: 2)

In today's mainstream conceptualization and practices of heritage, materiality or physicality is still attached crucial importance. Material remains are treated as the primary ground for testing heritage authenticity. For most critical heritage scholars, this privilege of materiality or material authenticity is a key feature of the AHD, whose origin can be traced back to European architectural conservation in the 19th century (Smith 2006; Waterton 2010; see also D'Agostino 2021; Swenson 2013). In contemporary China's system of heritage, material authenticity serves as a key criterion for the official recognition of heritage sites and a key issue in their preservation and management. Those that lack verifiable material authenticity are usually excluded from heritage recognition. Even when such sites are granted official status, they would soon become targets of criticism from both scholarly and public spheres.

Cultural reflections on the materiality-boundness of non-Western, especially Chinese and Asian, heritages have never stopped since the emergence of critical heritage studies (see, e.g., Byrne 1991, 2014; Chung 2005; Evers & Seagle 2012; Hou 2019; Lowenthal 1989; Rico 2016; Wu 2014b; Zhu 2024b). However, there are also some scholars critiquing these cultural voices as a form of binary thinking that presupposes and reinforces the West–East divide in heritage (e.g., Akagawa 2016; Gao & Jones 2021; Taylor 2015; Winter 2014). It is true that:

> in the West and the wider world, the idea and practice of heritage conservation has pluralised and expanded, with the boundaries between the tangible/intangible, material/social, human/non-human, art/craft becoming increasingly porous. [...] Asia has been part of a wider global trend. (Winter 2014: 133)

Nevertheless, it should be understood that this global trend of more pluralized heritage conceptualization and practice does not come from nowhere or a sudden epiphany. It is a result, at least partly, of the global development of critical heritage research and awareness that problematizes the materiality-centered discourse of heritage and its knowledge/ power, among which Asia's "discourse of difference" (Winter 2014) is a main contributing force. In other words, the "discourse of difference" from Asia or elsewhere has contributed to the diversification of heritage around the world, rather than harming the coexistence of Eastern and Western heritage ideas.

Should we now abandon this "discourse of difference" and other forms of it, as there is a global trend of heritage pluralization? It is not yet time for that. There is still a need for such discourses, and more nuanced and sophisticated expositions of the cultural differences in heritage to further promote this pluralizing trend. After all, in the World Heritage nomination process, the flow of expertise regarding technical or material issues is still of vital importance (James & Winter 2017). Furthermore, the AHD, featured by authenticity and materiality concerns, continues to exert significant influence on heritage practices across diverse cultural contexts – even in projects that ostensibly prioritize citizen participation (Pastor Pérez & Colomer 2024). In China, for example, it generates cultural effects such as spatial separation, emotional banishment, and value transformation, as well as instigating tensions between heritage agencies and local communities (Zhu 2015; see also Yan 2018; Zhu & Maags 2020). Furthermore, even lay people in China (especially urban China) have internalized this authenticity discourse. As Gao and Jones (2021: 99–100) report, there are numerous Chinese cases in which local residents dissent from actions in changing the physical existence of a heritage or express satisfaction over conservation efforts to maintain material authenticity. Though the two scholars take these Chinese cases as counterevidence to the "discourse of difference" between East and West in heritage thinking, I argue that they are, rather, illustrations of how influential the global, authorized discourse of authenticity is in contemporary China. As stated in Section 2, *guji*, as a Chinese cultural notion of heritage, has already been transformed by the modern, Western historical consciousness and, particularly, the AHD over the last century or so. One should not take for granted that Chinese people's understanding of heritage has not been affected by the globalized discourse.

Nonetheless, I should make it clear that I am not suggesting that the Chinese today should totally throw away their concerns over materiality or physicality when dealing with heritage. This is not only because the rapid urbanization process in contemporary China has been wiping out and endangering the physical existence of heritage at an alarming speed and scale, but also because the Chinese cultural discourse of *guji* would also consider physical dimensions. The role of materiality or physicality in Chinese *guji* discourse cannot be reduced to a yes or no assessment. One should ask: How was materiality or physicality understood and dealt with in the Chinese cultural discourse of *guji* before it was transformed by the globalized idea of heritage? How were the physical and material aspects of *guji* discursively represented or obscured, remembered or forgotten? Underlying such discursive representations, what cultural logic and meaning-making processes were at work? In this section, I attempt to offer some preliminary insights into these questions with my cultural-historical discourse analysis of the *guji* records in the seven local gazetteers of Quzhou.

Materiality Ignored to Foreground Cultural Associations

A notable pattern emerges from my discourse analysis of *guji* records across the seven local gazetteers of Quzhou is that the material or physical dimensions are very often excluded; foregrounded in those records are historical figures and their deeds associated with the *guji*. More specifically, almost all the succinct *guji* records in the seven local gazetteers of Quzhou are without any description of their physical aspects. In those lengthier records of *guji*, accounts of physical dimensions are not often seen, either. Here are a few examples for a more nuanced understanding of how the materiality/physicality of *guji* was (un)attended to or (dis)remembered.

> Example 3
> **The Yanxu Hotel** Located in the eastern part of the prefectural city. During the *Xiantong* reign (860–74) of the Tang dynasty, the prefect Zhao Lin gave a farewell dinner to his younger brother, the then prefect of Chuzhou – Zhao Zan – here.
>
> [**雁序馆** (在) 郡城西，唐咸通中刺史赵璘与其弟处州刺史瓒会别之所。]
> (Yang Zhun et al. 2009: 163; Lin et al. 2009: 398; Yao et al. 1970: 535; Zheng 1984: 750)

In this very brief documentation of the Yanxu Hotel as a *guji*, one cannot find any account of its physical existence. The most significant matter in this documentation is its once being a place where a memorable moment in the local past occurred, that is, in the late Tang dynasty, the prefect of Quzhou, Zhao Lin, gave a farewell dinner to his younger brother, Zhao Zan, who was then the prefect of Chuzhou (处州). Whatever reason(s) one may find for such nondescription of the physical being of this *guji*, it testifies that historical figures and their activities are far more important than the physical dimensions in the meaning-making of a *guji*, as it is the former respect that renders this particular hotel a memorable site and a site of memory.

> Example 4
> **The *Zhengmeng*[18] Pavilion** According to the *Xin'an Gazetteer*, Doulu Shu was previously named [Doulu] Fuzheng. When he was a youth, he once traveled to Quzhou. The prefect Zheng Shizhan said to him, "Your family name has two characters. It is not good that your given name is of two characters, too." He then wrote the character *shu* (署) and presented it to him. At night, the young man dreamed of an old man talking to him, "I heard that the prefect has changed your name. You'll get your fame taking the imperial exam four times. And twenty years after that, you'll be the prefect here. The man then pointed to a place, saying, "This place is good to build

---

[18] *Zhengmeng* (征梦) means that the dream is verified in real life.

a pavilion." Waking up, the young man changed his name to Shu. At that time, he had already failed the imperial examination twice. Taking the exam four times more, he succeeded and won his fame. Twenty years later, he was really appointed the prefect of Quzhou. Then he built this Zhengmeng Pavilion at the site the old man in his dream had pointed to him.

[征梦亭 按《信安志》：豆卢署初名辅真，少旅于衢，刺史郑式瞻谓曰："子复姓，不宜二名。"乃书署字授之。夕梦老父曰："闻使君与君易名，君当四举成名，后二十年牧兹郡。"指一地方曰："此处可建亭台。"既悟，因名署。时已再下第，又四举乃成名。后二十年果刺衢，于所指地立征梦亭。] (Lin et al. 2009: 398)

Notably, in this relatively lengthier record of the Zhengmeng Pavilion as a *guji*, its material existence is unheeded. What one reads is only an intriguing narrative of the pavilion's being built, in which the historical interaction between two prominent prefects of Quzhou, Doulu Shu and Zheng Shizhan, is foregrounded. Both of them were significant figures in the city's local history.

The Zhengmeng Pavilion is also found in other local gazetteers of Quzhou. Though even lengthier than the above documentation, one cannot find any account of its material or physical existence, either. In Shen's and Zhao's gazetteers, for example, this interesting narrative also constitutes the record of the Zhengmeng Pavilion as a *guji*, only that it has a few more details (Shen et al. 2009: 40; Yang et al. 2009: 161). In Yao's and Zheng's gazetteers, the documentation of the Zhengmeng Pavilion consists of the same story about how it had come to be built, and a couple of poems related to the pavilion (Yao et al. 1970: 544–45; Zheng 1984: 762) That is to say, the Quzhou local gazetteer compilers in different historical times did not consider its physical existence necessary to make meaning of the pavilion as a *guji*.

With this analysis, I want to further stress that the Chinese used not to care so much about materiality or physicality in remembering *guji*. The absence of physical or material considerations from *guji* records was commonplace. The examples analyzed earlier further provide support from a cultural-historical perspective for scholars who maintain that the Chinese idea of heritage is not materiality-bounded (e.g., Hou & Wu 2012; Lowenthal 1989; Ruan & Lin 2003; Wu 2012b; Yu 2008, 2012). It is important to note, however, that this observation should not be interpreted as a support for the claim that Chinese – or, more broadly, Asian – cultures place greater value on intangible heritage than on tangible heritage. I remain unconvinced by such a view. As I have contended in the previous section, this dichotomous grouping of heritage is misaligned with the cultural-historical conception of *guji*, and the Chinese *yin–yang* philosophy. What I am showing here is that the material or physical facts were not often an issue in the recognition and meaning-making of *guji* that we today tend to classify as tangible heritage. In other words, even in dealing with what is today called tangible heritage, the Chinese used not to care too much about its material or physical aspects. It seems that the Chinese well understood that "all heritage is intangible" long before Smith (2006: 3; 2011: 11) made this claim. For them, a *guji* was meaningful and memorable because it sustained "a performance or cultural process" (Smith 2011: 11) through which the past was translated to be a valuable resource in the present. Even though its material existence was lost, a *guji* could continue to fulfill its function, so long as this cultural process remained active. In such cases, tracing the site where the *guji* once physically stood became especially significant.

Tracing the Site

Intimately pertinent to the issue of materiality or physicality, site stands out to be an overarching concern in the *guji* discourse, as revealed in the Quzhou local gazetteers under inspection. It should be explained at once that the idea of site in the Chinese *guji* discourse is different from how we perceive it in the contemporary system of heritage. Today, sites constitute a particular type of tangible heritage, defined as "works of man or the combined works of nature and man, and areas including archaeological sites which are of outstanding universal value from the historical, aesthetic, ethnological or anthropological point of view" (UNESCO 1972: 2). Unlike monuments or built heritages, sites do not have those structures standing as they were in material integrity; there are only material remains on and/or under the ground to authenticate their status as heritage. The enlisted world heritages of this type in China include the Peking Man Site at Zhoukoudian, the Yin Xu and the Site of Xanadu. Arguably, these sites have been recognized because they best exemplify the universal values in the AHD framework, based on archeological research of the material remains excavated. In the Third National Survey of Immovable Heritage (Quzhou), no registration of a site as such is identified. This indicates that in Quzhou there are no sites that demonstrate universal heritage values, or, rather, no material remnants for the state-sanctioned heritage surveyors to authenticate a site of universal heritage values. However, when a historically significant space or structure collapsed, how might its site be treated in the cultural discourse of *guji*? Through examining the *guji* records in Quzhou's seven local gazetteers, I explicate alternative ways of conceptualizing and remembering sites, so as to illuminate distinct understandings of materiality or physicality within the marginalized Chinese *guji* discourse.

First, a structure or place of historic significance could be recognized and remembered as *guji* after its physical destruction or desolation, whether its site could be determined or not. For example,

Example 5
The Yuefeng Pavilion Located behind the seat of the prefectural government. It was built in the seventh year of the Jiajing (1528) by the prefect Sir Wang. Today, it is desolated.

[乐丰亭 在府治后,嘉靖七年郡守王公建,今废。][19]

Despite its state of desolation at the time of its documentation, the pavilion retained its status as *guji*. In this record, what comes first is the original location or the site where the pavilion used to stand. Actually, as may be noticed in the examples presented earlier, most *guji* records begin with a description of where it is or was standing. This indicates the crucial significance of the location or site of *guji* in the Chinese cultural thinking.

Example 6
The Demolished Yingchuan County (*Taiping Huanyu Ji*) 95 *li*[20] south from the prefectural city. (*Fanyu Jiyao*) 90 *li* south from the prefectural city [...]. (The previous gazetteer) The site of the city seems to be still there ....

[盈川废县 (太平寰宇记) 在州南九十五里 (方舆纪要) 州南九十里 [......] (旧志) 城址仿佛犹存。 ......] (Yao et al. 1970: 530–31)

In this record of the Demolished Yingchuan County as a *guji*, the exact location of the site is left uncertain. It seems that the local gazetteer compilers at the time had no sufficient physical evidence to determine where it used to stand. They offered two versions for this, by quoting historical documentation from a book completed in the late 10th century, *Taiping huanyu ji* (Universal Geography of the Taiping Era) and one published in 1692, *Fanyu jiyao* (Essence of Historical Geography). These two versions of site location have a discrepancy of five *li* or 2.5 kilometers between them. It should be observed that the second version is in smaller-sized characters, suggesting that the local gazetteer compilers consider it less accurate than the first one.

What runs after these two versions of site location in the *guji* record is another quotation from the previous county gazetteer, that is, Chen's gazetteer compiled in 1699, stating that "the site of the city seems to be still there." This indicates that the compilers of Chen's gazetteer had traced a site for the Demolished Yingchuan County, yet were uncertain or unable to authenticate that it was. They added the hedge word "仿佛" (*fangfu*, seems to) to confess their uncertainty. This indeterminacy was then carried over by the compilers of Yao's gazetteer, who simply retained Chen's equivocal conclusion without resolving

---

[19] Chen Pengnian陈鹏年 (supervised), Xu Zhikai徐之凯 et al. (compiled), *Xi'an County Gazetteer* [西安县志], Kangxi 18th year version, vol. 3.
[20] *Li* (里) is a Chinese measurement of distance. One *li* equals to 500 meters.

the ambiguity surrounding the *guji*'s precise whereabouts. From Sima Qian's perspective, this is to pass down the uncertainty as uncertainty (Sima 1959: 487), without affecting the recognition and remembrance of it as a *guji*.

Second, a collapsed structure could be a *guji* even though its site was already untraceable. For the then Chinese, it was not necessarily a *guji* lost that allowed disremembering, nor was it problematic to announce that its site could not be verified. Arguably, the traceability of a site in the physical world was not a critical factor in determining whether a *guji* could be recognized or not. Here are a couple of examples for illustration.

> Example 7
> **The Hefeng Post** Built in the Shaoxing reign (1131–62) of the Song dynasty by the prefect Sir Zhang, who was born in *Xiangyang*. It had long been abandoned. <u>Its base and site cannot be found.</u>
>
> [和风驿 宋绍兴中郡守襄阳张公建, 废久, <u>基址无可考</u>。][21]

As underlined, this entry of the Hefeng Post as a *guji* explicitly states that it had been abandoned, and its site was no longer verifiable at the time when it was documented in the local gazetteer. Nonetheless, this did not affect its value or meaningfulness to be recorded as a *guji*. In so doing, the local gazetteer compilers at least granted people in their time and the coming ages a chance to transmit the name of this post. More importantly, this recognition and documentation of it as a *guji* could work to transmit the name and memory of Sir Zhang, a prefect of Quzhou in the 12th century, encouraging contemporary and future officials in Quzhou to build such useful infrastructures so as to make their names remembered by later generations.

> Example 8
> **The Chuangshan Pavilion, the Yuepo Pavilion, the Fengyue Pavilion**
>
> <u>Their bases, sites and histories of establishment and desolation are all untraceable.</u>
>
> [闯山亭 月坡亭 风月亭 <u>基址兴废俱不可考</u>。][22]

Captivatingly, the three pavilions recorded in this *guji* entry seem to have nothing traceable, their sites included. Though so, they could still be *guji*, worthwhile to be documented and made known to the present and later generations. The only thing transmitted is their names. Indeed, names can serve as a memorial form to be called and recalled. This aligns with Azaryahu's (2021: 1) conceptualization of "onymic commemoration," that is, a complex

---

[21] Chen Pengnian 陈鹏年 (supervised), Xu Zhikai 徐之凯 et al. (compiled), (1699). *Xi'an County Gazetteer* [西安县志], Kangxi 38th year version, the introductory volume.

[22] Chen et al., *Xi'an County Gazetteer*, 1699.

process that operates via the remembrance of, by, and through, names, as "a time-honored and prestigious technology of immortality."

What cultural imperative drove the Chinese practice of recognizing and remembering *guji* without physical remains or traceable sites? Did they really attempt to remember every desolated, disappeared *guji*, or every empty or even untraceable site? In the *Fanli* of Zhao's gazetteer, whose chapter of *guji* includes similar records of the Hefeng Post and the three pavilions named earlier, a clear clue to answer those questions is found. It reads:

> Those that have been demolished today and without verifiable sites will be omitted. Though demolished, some *guji*, such as the Hefeng Post, the Chuangshan Pavilion and so on, will still be recorded, rather than deleted. This is to pass down the words or writings of renowned figures. [今废, 址俱不可考, 故削之。虽废, 如和风驿、闯山亭之类犹存而弗削者, 存名人之辞翰也。] (Yang et al. 2009: 164)

Clearly, this statement shows that the Chinese did permit forgetting *guji* when their sites were no longer traceable. However, the overriding principle governing whether a *guji* could be disremembered was not the traceability of its site, but whether it could still serve to transmit the words or writings of memorable human figures. The deep cultural thinking behind this is, as discussed in Section 2, that the idea of *guji* used to privilege the transmission of *words, especially poetic words, and the memory of human figures*. For the Chinese, "[t]he past was a past of words, not of stones" (Mote 1973: 51). Wu (2012) advocates the idea of "language authenticity" for Chinese heritage. That is, language should be taken as a key aspect in maintaining the authenticity of heritage in China. It is more important to preserve and transmit authentic language than material or other matters in Chinese heritage practices (see also Hou et al. 2019).

Third, the process of tracing where the site of a *guji* is itself important or meaningful to be documented. In the seven local gazetteers of Quzhou under inspection, multiple *guji* entries specify the compilers' efforts to identify and demarcate sites. This practice is particularly well illustrated in Yao's gazetteer's account of the *Fushi* (Floating Stone) Pavilion:

> Example 9
> **The Fushi Pavilion** Located at the Fushi Ferry outside the Gongcheng Gate. In studying earlier gazetteers, I encountered Meng Jiao's poem about the Lanke Stone at Zhengrong Ridge. Later, upon reading the collected works of Meng Jiao, I found a poem of the Fushi Pavilion, which raised doubts about whether its site was at the previously stated location. However, upon examining the collected works of Zhao Qianxian, I discovered references that "the Fushi Immortal's trace is at the finishing stone along the river beside my house," and that "the Fushi Immortal's trace still remains." When considering these

together with the final lines of Meng's poem, I could confirm its site is indeed there. Yet surprisingly, earlier gazetteers omit any mention of the Fushi Immortal; the story appears only in these two respected figures' poems. People have all been speaking of the legend of the Lanke Mountain, yet few know about this tale. Are deities also destined to be or not to be transmitted? ...

[**浮石亭** 在拱辰门外浮石渡。尝考旧志,有孟郊峥嵘岭烂柯石诗,后读郊集又得浮石亭诗, 或恐非此地。因读赵清献集, 有浮石仙人遗迹在吾庐江畔钓鱼矶, 又浮石仙人迹尚存, 合之郊诗结语, 知其为此地也。独怪浮石仙人事前志不载, 仅见于二公诗。世竞传柯山事而知此者寥寥, 岂仙人传不传亦有数耶? ......] (Yao et al. 1970: 545–46)

This record of the Fushi Pavilion as a *guji* is primarily a narrative of how the site of it was traced textually. The compiler's examination of a poem about this *guji* written by the esteemed Tang-dynasty poet Meng Jiao (孟郊, 751–814) raised doubts about the recorded site of this *guji*. Further inspection into the collected works of Zhao Qingxian or better known as Zhao Bian (赵抃, 1008-84) – a celebrated Song-dynasty scholar–official who was born, grew up and lived his retired life in Quzhou, coupled with a close analysis of the concluding lines of Meng Jiao's poem, confirmed that the site documentation was right. Rather than simply the finding, this site-tracing journey was also presented to the readers, so as to unfold a process of recollecting *gu* (稽古, *jigu*). As I have previously expounded on, in traditional Chinese cultural thinking, "recollecting *gu* is [a means to be] in accordance with heaven." That might be the reason why this journey of site tracing was deemed worthy of documentation.

Furthermore, it can be inferred that the site of the Fushi Pavilion was no longer physically identifiable at the time, as the process of locating and documenting the site relied entirely on textual sources. This lack of physical evidence, however, did not affect its status as a *guji*, for its significance was tied to the words of renowned historical figures and traces of deities. The gazetteer compiler also expressed surprise – or, rather, discontent – at the omission of the Fushi Immortal's tale in earlier Quzhou gazetteers. As discussed in Section 2, this tale can be a crucial source of meaning-making for the Fushi Pavilion as a *guji*.

Another example of illustrative power is the entry of the Zhuangyuan Torii[23] in Zheng's gazetteer. As the documentation goes:

Example 10
The Zhuangyuan Torii (*Jiaqing County Gazetteer*). It was built for Liu Mengyan, Chen Su, Mao Zizhi, etc.

---

[23] *Zhuangyuan* (状元) was the title for the one who won the first place in the highest level of the imperial examinations – a national system of examination to select officials.

Note: This torii collapsed a long time ago. Only this name has survived. It was at the end of *Mazhan*, south from the *Wu* Bridge. *Zhan* (栈) is vernacularly written as *zhan* (站). According to local seniors, this site is actually the house where the *zhuangyuan* Liu Mengyan had lived, and Mazhan was the stable where Liu Mengyan fed horses. ...

[**状元坊** (嘉庆县志) 为留梦炎、程宿、毛自知等立。
按: 此坊久圮, 仅存其名, 在乌桥南马栈底, 栈俗作站, 然据故老相传其地实留状元故居, 马栈亦留状元当年厮养所也。 ......] (Zheng 1984: 717–18)

While the torii had long since collapsed, the site might be lost to time. The local gazetteer compiler Zheng Yongxi then sought to rediscover it by interviewing local seniors. This process of site tracing is discernible from Zheng's note in the entry, particularly his representation of the voice of local seniors. With help from them, Zheng traced more than the site of the Zhuangyuan Torii. He further found that Liu Mengyan's house and stable used to be at this site as well.

To conclude this analysis, I would like to reiterate that site held critical importance in the Chinese cultural discourse of *guji*. However, unlike today's mainstream heritage conceptualization, the concern over sites in premodern Chinese thinking was not so much about conserving material remains in the designated space as about transmitting memories—those about particular historical figures and their words, even those deity tales or simply names that had been left. Often, the site of a *guji* was empty, lacking any physical traces that could be subjected to what is today called authenticity tests. Later generations would employ various methods to locate such sites, including textual research, fieldwork interviews, and others. These efforts might yield inconclusive results, and, in some cases, nothing at all. Even in such instances, however, documenting the lost *guji* remained evocative, and the process of tracing its site was itself meaningful. Such documentation can illuminate a process of recollecting *gu*, or efforts to reconnect with and meaningfully reinterpret the past in the present.

The Meaning-Making of Physicality

A close examination of the seven local gazetteers of Quzhou also reveals that the physical aspects of *guji* were occasionally incorporated into the records, though they were more often than not neglected. How did local historians of Quzhou frame or portray the material or physical aspects of a *guji*? In what ways did their documentation of material facets converge with or diverge from our modern heritage discourse? What cultural processes of meaning-making shaped these material accounts? These questions remain largely unexplored, as scholarly discourse has typically focused on either defending or challenging the idea that Chinese heritage approaches transcend the concern over materiality or material authenticity. In this subsection, I address these questions through examining two *guji* cases, the Official Seat of the Magistrate Assistant, and the Office of the Judicial Assistant, as recorded in Zheng's gazetteer.

The records of the two *guji* read as follows.

> Example 11
>
> **The Official Seat of the Magistrate Assistant** (*Jiaqing County Gazetteer*) Located initially at the eastern side of the retreat hall in the county's official seat. In the 41st year of the Qianlong reign (1752), it was detached and relocated at the Zhangshutan in the eastern city. The magistrate assistant Yang Xiang built this official seat, whose hall had three principal columns. At the right and the left sides of it, there were porches. Behind the hall was the interior house of three rooms. In front of the hall were the main gate and the screen wall. During the *Xianfeng* reign (1851–61), this official seat was destroyed during a war. . . .
>
> [县丞署 (嘉庆县志) 原在县署退堂东。乾隆四十一年分防城东樟树潭, 县丞杨翔建署, 为堂三楹, 左右有廊, 后有内宅三楹, 堂前为大门、为屏墙。咸丰兵毁。 ......] (Zheng 1984: 711)

> Example 12
>
> **The Office of the Judicial Assistant** (*Kangxi County Gazetteer*). The Judicial Assistant's Office is located east of the Zhong'ai Hall in the county seat, south of the Assistant Magistrate's residence. The Assistant Magistrate's office is known as the Grain Yamen, while the Judicial Assistant's office is also called the Constabulary Yamen. (Jiaqing County Gazetteer) The Judicial Assistant's residence is situated at the northwestern edge of the county seat. In the middle is a hall, with a two-bay corridor to its east. Behind this were two halls, and further back is the inner residence of five bays. West of the main hall stands a three-bay study, while a ceremonial gate is positioned to the hall's south.
>
> [典史厅 (康熙县志) 县治忠爱堂之东为典史厅, 在县丞之宅南, 丞称粮衙, 典史亦称捕衙。(嘉庆县志) 县治西进迤北为典史宅, 中为堂, 堂东有廊二楹, 后为二堂, 更后为内宅五楹, 堂西有书室三楹, 堂南为仪门。]
> (Zheng 1984: 711)

As underlined, these two *guji* records do have accounts of their physical erection. Observably, these physical accounts focus on the architectural structure of the two official buildings, with little attention given to specific details or micro-level architectural characteristics. This form of physical documentation stands in stark contrast to the expectations of modern heritage specialists, who would seek more information on, for example, the precise dimensions of the structures and their components, the materials used, the architectural styles and aesthetic principles embodied, as well as the construction techniques and levels of technical sophistication involved.

To better illustrate this, one efficacious strategy is to compare these *guji* records with contemporary heritage documentation. Here is how a "Zhejiang Provincial Key Unit of Cultural Heritage" in Quzhou, the Tianfei Gong (literally Heavenly Queen Palace), is recorded in the Third National Survey of Immovable Heritage in 2009. In the registration form of this heritage, an introduction to it goes as follows:

> The Heavenly Queen Palace is located at No.18, Tianhuang Alley. It was built to commemorate the Heavenly Queen – Mazu, and thus also called Heavenly Queen Palace. This architecture occupies the east and faces the west. At first, it was 2,052.9 square meters in size. Today, only 650.89 square meters remain. In horizontal layout, it appears like a vertical rectangle. It has two side doors in the northern and southern parts of its front wall. Over the main gate, there is a stone plaque that reads "*Tian Hou Gong*." The main gate faces 20 degrees north of due west. 15.75 meters westward from the main gate is a screen wall. Going through the main gate, one enters its front hall. Moving inward further is a yard, with two wings (*xianglou*) at its south and north. The ground of the yard is covered with flagstones. Right in the middle of it, a corridor cuts through and connects to the main hall. Another section (*jin*) behind the main hall was pulled down. The front hall is built upon a stone base of two layers. Above the main gate are brick carvings. They are mainly in the shape of 片, scattered around which are images of human beings, birds and beasts, of trees and stones, and of landscapes. During the Cultural Revolution (1967–77), these brick carvings were covered by yellow mud. The front hall is of five *jian* and two floors. The second floor is the stage for Chinese opera performance. [. . .] The architecture is basically well preserved. The brick carvings over the main gate are delicately beautiful. The *dougong, queti, tuojiao*, etc., in the architecture are mostly engraved; the engravings are fine, delicate, and dense, with golden light and varied colors shining, but the overall images of them look dull, being clearly of the late Qing style.[24]

As clearly seen, this documentation of the Heavenly Queen Palace as a heritage is predominantly about its physical existence. The state-sanctioned heritage surveyors have offered thorough and detailed accounts of how the Heavenly Queen Palace looks like in physical and material terms and how it was constructed, including information about its size, layout, structure, fabric, its construction materials, techniques, decoration style and aesthetics. Perceptibly, these descriptions are to demonstrate the so-called universal values (scientific, historic, and aesthetic) of this built heritage. Scientifically, the Heavenly Queen Palace is depicted as an

---

[24] This document was provided by the Quzhou local authority of culture and tourism in Chinese.

architectural building with fine design and careful structural and constructional contemplations, so that it can be regarded as a human creation with scientific and technological complexity. Historically, the Heavenly Queen Palace is represented as a piece of architecture of the late Qing era, surviving the drastic transformations in late imperial and modern Chinese history. Aesthetically, the architectural style and decoration details are underscored to portray the Heavenly Queen Palace as a work of architectural art. Though the images of the engravings look dull (from an architectural art point of view), they reflect the aesthetic style and taste in late Qing China.

With this analytical observation in mind, I turn back to the two records of Quzhou official buildings as *guji*. Though the physical description constitutes a notable part in each of the records, it is much less prominent than that in the contemporary heritage documentation as exemplified earlier. To understand such less detailed accounts of *guji* physicality, we should not follow contemporary heritage or architectural perspectives. As many scholars have pointed out, architecture in imperial China, especially royal palaces and official seats, had been shaped by family-state politics and, more fundamentally, Chinese *Li* (礼) thinking (Li 2020; Zhang 2011). *Li*, as "the determinate fabric of Chinese culture" (Hall & Ames 1998: 269), does not have a single equivalent term in the English language. As Chard (2011: 29) summarizes, it has been translated into words such as "ritual, rites, ceremonial, etiquette, manners, rules of behavior, ritual propriety," or, more generally, "prescriptive rules or norms which govern society." As colleagues and I have contended elsewhere, *Li* is a guiding discourse that shapes the meaning-making of Chinese heritage or *guji* in premodern times (Hou & Wu 2017: 83–4; Wu & Yao 2014). Furthermore, Peng Zhaorong (2018) has highlighted the primordial role of *Li* to understand Chinese intangible heritage.

In the description of the two official seats as *guji*, this Chinese cultural understanding was perceptibly embedded. First, the principle "*qian tang hou shi*" (the audience hall is in the front and the rooms are in the back) or "*qian ya hou qin*" (the office is in the front and the living space is in the back) had been observed when building the two official seats. This was the basic scheme of architectural construction in traditional China, guided by the *Li* discourse. It can be traced back to the ancient Chinese classics of *Li*. For example, while commenting on the *Yili* (*Book of Etiquette and Rites*), the Qing official–scholar Sheng Shizuo (盛世佐, 1719–55) affirmed that "the scheme for architecture is *qian tang hou shi*."[25]

Furthermore, the physical descriptions of the two official architecture as *guji* show a concern over scale, another important dimension of the Chinese *Li*

---

[25] Sheng Shizuo 盛世佐, *Assembling Yili Commentaries* [仪礼集编], *Wenyuange Complete Library in the Four Branches of Literature* version, vol. 6.

discourse that shapes the meaning-making of architecture, because it is through the distinction in scale that *Li* forges itself. As stated in the *Li Ki* (*Book of Rites*),

> In some ceremonial usages, the multitude of things formed the mark of distinction. The son of Heaven had 7 shrines in his ancestral temple; the prince of a state, 5; Great officers, 3; and other officers, 1. (*Li Ki*, 10: 7; Legge's translation 1885: 397)
>
> In others, greatness of size formed the mark. The dimensions of palaces and apartments; the measurements of dishes and (other) articles ... (*Li Ki*, 10: 9; Legge's translation 1885: 399) ...

The official seats should meet the requirements of *Li* at the time it was constructed. In late imperial China, according to Tian Kai (2012: 108), the main hall of the official seat for officials ranked from the ninth to the sixth levels ought to have three rooms. The magistrate assistant of a county outside of the provincial capital was in the eighth rank, and the judicial assistant of a county was rankless. When the Chinese read such physical descriptions in premodern days, they would judge whether these buildings were appropriate in terms of *Li*: The Office of the Magistrate Assistant was an appropriate one, while the Office of the Judicial Assistance was not, as its scale was even larger than the Office of the Magistrate Assistant. This can be understood as a different politics of the past in the present. It functioned as a mirror for the local officials at that time to reflect on their own behaviors in using building (and more) and thereby guide their future deeds.

In light of this discourse analysis of *guji*, some of the assumptions and limitations that underlie contemporary heritage identification and management practices need to be reflected on. Typically, when the material remains of a historically significant site are no longer extant, one tends to deny its status of heritage. The response is often limited to expressions of regret and blame: They lament that the site was not properly preserved and reproach institutions or individuals for their failure to protect it. Ironically, this is usually followed by collective forgetting. Behind such a tendency is a deep entrenchment in the Western-originated conception of heritage authenticity. It should be stressed, however, that loss is not equivalent to nonexistence. A site may no longer possess physical remains or traces, but this does not necessarily preclude its value as heritage. Having no material remnants or even lost traces of the site, a heritage may still be valuable and memorable, if it has a poetic writing, a tale, or simply a name left.

The debate on heritage materiality/physicality also needs further reflections, as our contemporary perspectives, including those who critique the East–West binary or the "discourse of difference" in heritage thinking, remain constrained by Western-originated dichotomies and disciplinary frameworks. Basically, the current debate operates largely within a yes–no dichotomy in thinking and rethinking heritage materiality or physicality. However, the issue can be much more complicated. For example, can one interpret the Chinese concern over the site of *guji* as a concern over its materiality? One cannot simply say yes or no. As I have shown, the Chinese had enthusiastically researched and recorded where the physical site of a *guji* was, but if they could not physically verify the site, it would not matter so much. Furthermore, we need to ask: When people show concerns over heritage materiality or physically, what are they really concerned about? In today's mainstream heritage discourse and practice, such concerns are usually directed to the so-called "innate values" in science, technology, art, and history. Nevertheless, these values are not really innate but are assigned by heritage experts from their disciplinary (archeological, architectural, artistic, or historical) perspectives. In contrast, the premodern Chinese engagement with the physicality of a *guji* was usually from the perspective of *Li*, a different politics of the past in the present. This alerts us that the concern over heritage materiality or physicality might have divergent meanings and implications across cultures and time. Heritage researchers and practitioners should carefully examine this, rather than instinctively bring in their own disciplinary knowledge to understand materiality or physicality in heritage work.

5 *Guji* in a Holistic View

> Stepping into a new territory for travel or sightseeing, one first asks about the sages and wise figures of bygone eras, seeks for the great events occurred in history, and talks to locals to trace the sites associated with them. A hall or a pavilion may conjure the elegance of a hundred years past; a derelict temple or an ancient tomb may recall heroes ten centuries ago. Even though those ruined sites, by the emptiness they left we may still commemorate the past. Never fade are their names and auras, which will inspire us in days to come. [入境游观，先询往哲，追前胜事，聊访遗踪。月榭风亭，犹想百年光霁；荒祠古墓，回思千载英灵。虽废址，堪悲空吊往古，而流芳未泯，可激来今。] (Lin et al. 2009: 398)

In the preceding sections, I have selectively foregrounded particular aspects of the Chinese *guji* discourse to facilitate a clear exposition of its main ways of meaning-making and remembering the past. Nevertheless, as readers may have noticed, these aspects do not exist in isolation; rather, they frequently intersect and coalesce within individual instances of *guji* documentation. In this final analytical section, I hope to provide a more holistic understanding of the Chinese *guji* discourse. What I choose to do is a focused analysis of a single, emblematic case – the House of Yin Hao (殷浩宅). This case analysis will enable revisiting the earlier themes addressed while bringing their interrelations into sharper relief, thus offering a more cohesive elucidation of how this forgotten Chinese discourse of heritage operated in ways different from the AHD.

Yin Hao (殷浩, 303–55) was a renowned military general in the Eastern Jin dynasty (317–420), whose deeds were well documented in the *Book of Jin* (see Fang et al. 1974: 2043–49). He spent his later years in Quzhou and was buried there after his death. Yin Hao has been regarded as an important figure in the local history, with stories and traces of his life in Quzhou meticulously recorded in the local gazetteers. My analysis of the House of Yin Hao as a *guji* will draw on the records from Yao's and Zheng's gazetteers. These two are chosen for the reason that, as shall soon be evident, they reproduce the documentation of this *guji* in other local gazetteers of Quzhou. To examine them will not blind us from seeing how it was recorded and understood across time.

Now let us look at the record of the House of Yin Hao in Yao's gazetteer, which goes as follows:

> Example 13–1
> **The House of Yin Hao** (*Yuanfeng Gazetteer of the Nine Regions of China*) Located in the Xi'an County. The base of the house is still there. Locals call it Yinqiang (the wall of the Yin family). (*Tianqi Prefecture Gazetteer of Quzhou*) Located in the Xin'an Old City, 6 *li* south to the Xi'an County. Hao was the Mid General in the Jin dynasty. During the Jianyuan reign (343–44), he was defeated in the northern expedition by Yao Xiang. For that reason, he was removed from office and relegated to layperson. He was sent to live here. Its site still exists, and by the roadside there is a small stone chamber, housing a statue of a deity whose image is a warrior in helmet and armor . . . .
> [殷浩宅 (元丰九域志) 在西安县, 基地犹存。土人号曰殷墙。(天启府志) 在西安县南六里信安故城, 浩在晋为中将军, 建元间北伐为姚襄所败, 废为庶人, 贬居于此。其址犹存, 道旁有小石室, 其神为介胄之像。……]
> (Yao B. et al. 1970: 567–68)

First, this record of the House of Yin Hao as a *guji* exhibits little concern over its material existence, as there are no descriptions of its physical appearance, structure, or remnants. One can argue that this absence of physical description might be due to the long-ago demolition of the house, which prevented the local gazetteer compilers from providing any details about its material form. While this could be true, it is noteworthy that the compilers did not cite physical descriptions of the house from the *Yuanfeng Gazetteer of the Nine Regions of China* or the *Tianqi Prefectural Gazetteer of Quzhou*. They either could not locate any in these early historical writings or deemed it meaningless to include such information. Whatever the reason was, it is safe to say that the material characteristics of the house were not deemed of much significance in the *guji* discourse then. Thus, even though the House of Yin Hao had long been demolished or materially gone, it was still recorded and remembered as a *guji* in Quzhou.

Second, the issue of site was a serious concern in this entry of the House of Yin Hao as a *guji*. The local gazetteer compilers brought together two historical records to speak of this *guji*, both of which mentioned the site of the fallen house. According to the *Yuanfeng Gazetteer of the Nine Areas of China*, which was compiled during the Yuanfeng reign (1078–85) of the Song dynasty, the base of the house was visible in the 11th century, referred to by locals as Yinqiang (Walls of the Yin). This might suggest that the collapsed walls of the house were also discernible then. By the early Ming dynasty, as noted in Shen's gazetteer compiled in the 1500s, only the site itself was traceable. Through these quoted historical records, the local gazetteer compilers not only provided the essential information about the fallen house and its historical changes, but also suggested that tracing the site was a long-lasting tradition in the recording and remembering of *guji*. Such an act, as indicated in this entry, happened in different times of history in dealing with the House of Yin Hao as a *guji*.

Third, the life story of Yin Hao constitutes a very, if not the most important, part in the documentation and meaning-making of this collapsed house as a *guji*. Essentially, it is because of him that this fallen house or empty site of it has been deemed valuable and memorable. Despite his defeat as a general, Yin Hao was a person of virtue and reputation (see, e.g., Fang et al. 1974: 2043–49; Yao et al. 1970: 1424–25). The mere fact that such a historical figure had once resided therein transformed this house into a memorable *guji*, even after the physical structure had vanished. In other words, the significance of this site derives not from its material remnants but from its association with the life trajectory of a noteworthy historical figure.

Fourth, the local belief is rendered pertinent to this site to commemorate Yin Hao, as in the Chinese discourse of *guji*, the liaisons with human and/or divine figures were its primary sources of meaning. In this entry of *guji*, one encounters an account of the local worship of a warrior deity. While definitive evidence connecting this deity to Yin Hao is not provided, the inclusion of this description under the entry of the House of Yin Hao opens up ample possibilities toward this interpretation. This account of local belief, it can be argued, enriches the *guji* with an added layer of meaning, and creates space for further negotiation and imagination of its significance.

In the entry of the House of Yin Hao in Zheng's gazetteer, what is recorded in Yao's gazetteer is fully reiterated, with some additional details and stories supplemented. By examining this fuller *guji* record, I can further illustrate the Chinese idea of what is now called "heritage."

Example 13–2

The House of Yin Hao (*The General Gazetteer of the Great Ming*) Located south to the prefectural city. Hao was an officer in the Eastern Jin dynasty. During the Jianyuan reign (343–44), he was defeated in the northern expedition by Yao Xiang and was thus dismissed from office and relegated to layperson. He was further punished to move to Xin'an and live in this house. Its site still remains, which is called Yinqiang (the walls of the Yin). The General Gazetteer of Qing: 6 *li* south from the Xi'an County. Hao was dismissed from office and sent here after his defeat at Mount Sang. (*Guangxuji*) Hao was removed from his position and moved to *Xin'an*. Every day, he wrote in the air four characters – *duo duo guai shi* (truly very unreasonable matter). His nephew Han Bo accompanied him to this place. A year later, Bo chose to go back to the capital. Hao saw him off to the river, reciting Cao Yanhuan's poetic lines, "When one enjoys position and wealth, others come to send warmth; when one drops into poverty and doggery, relatives leave to augment misery." With this, he wept (*Kangxi County Gazetteer*). Hao was the Middle General in the Jin dynasty. Defeated in a battle, he was dismissed from office and moved to Xin'an. He had not a word of complaint. The house he had lived in was desolated later. The locals call the site Yinqiang. To eschew the taboo of referring to an emperor, it was changed to be Qingqiang. This should be in the Song dynasty. A long time later, it was transformed into the Longshou Temple. Beside the road, there is a stone case, inside which a statue of a deity wearing a helmet and armour is seen. Zhao's gazetteer says that there remains the base of the Temple of the General. This is because Yin's old official residence bore the title of General. Today, 6 *li* south of the county is a Temple of the General, which might be the site of Yin Hao's house, but the locals reckon it was [a temple built] for another general.

In the Tang-dynasty scholar-official Xue Feng's poem "Seeing off Mr. Cui from Quzhou," a line reads "the red tree covers silently the House of Yin Hao." The Qing scholar Mao Qiling's poem *To nephew Tian When Passing by the House of Yin Hao in Xin'an*: the day when Yin Hao moved to the south, not a company among relatives or friends. Today, I passed by the house of Yin Hao, tears shed while thinking of his nephew Han.

[**殷浩宅** (明一统志) 在府城南。浩仕东晋，建元间北伐为姚襄所败，废为庶人，贬信安居此。其址犹存，号曰殷墙。清统志: 在西安县南六里信安故城，浩以山桑之败贬此。（广舆记）浩废信安，终日书空作"咄咄怪事"四字。甥韩伯随至徙所，经岁还都，浩送之江上，咏曹颜还诗云: "富贵他人合，贫贱亲戚离。"因而泣下。（康熙县志）浩仕晋，为中将军，败废徙居信安，口无怨言。后宅废，土人名其处曰殷墙。因避讳改曰庆墙 当在宋代。久之为龙寿寺，道旁有小石室，其神为介胄之像 赵志云有将军庙基，盖殷官有将军号故也。今城南六里有将军殿，或即其址，但土人以为别一将军。

唐薛逢送衢州崔员外诗有"红树暗藏殷浩宅"句。清毛奇龄《过新安殷浩宅示田甥》诗: 当年殷浩南迁日，无复亲知相伴行，今日一过殷浩宅，叫人流涕对韩甥。] (Zheng 1984: 744)

As seen here, there are three main embellishments in the latter record of the House of Yin Hao. First, it includes an extra quotation from *Guangyuji* (*The Records of Vast Territories*), a historic-geographical work compiled by the late Ming scholar Lu Yingyang (陆应阳, 1542–1624). This quotation tells Yin Hao's story in a fuller fashion, from which one is not only informed of Yin Hao's miserable relocation to Quzhou but also episodes of his dejected life in this house. This nuanced depiction enriches the cultural meaning associated with the site, inviting resonances with and reflections on the present society or one's personal experiences. Furthermore, the story has the potential to evoke sympathy for Yin Hao among present and future generations, whether through reading this *guji* documentation or visiting the site with this story in mind. This emotional bond across time finds further expression in other parts of the *guji* record.

Second, this entry of the House of Yin Hao includes some lines from two poems that are absent in Yao's gazetteer. The first poem, specifically a line from it, was written by the Tang dynasty literati-official Xue Feng (薛逢, ca. 806–74). The inclusion of this verse referencing the House of Yin Hao indicates at least that this *guji* was both recognizable and significant in the 9th century. The other poem, written by the Qing-dynasty scholar Mao Qiling (毛奇龄, 1623–1716), is reproduced in its full length in the documentation, from which one can see how this *guji* could provoke emotions and sentiments. In reading the poetic lines Mao Qiling wrote to his nephew surnamed Tian, one would sense the poignant feelings that the poet had when he passed by this *guji*, a site of memory that accommodates stories of Yin Hao and especially the story that his nephew Han Bo accompanied him here yet chose to leave him after staying for a year. He could empathize with what Yin Hao had felt when seeing off his nephew. As discussed in the second section, such empathy across time is of key importance in the meaning-making of *guji*.

Furthermore, these two poems contribute to rendering the House of Yin Hao a site of *xing* – or a site of poetics (Hou 2019). This transformation occurs as the house is imbued with meaning in past poetic compositions while summoning new poetic responses. Mao Qiling's verses, written to his nephew as he passed by the site, convey a strong emotional resonance that ties the present moment he was in to the memory of the past. Once incorporated into the textual history of the *guji*, Mao's poem becomes part of an evolving process of meaning-making, open to new interpretations, and invites readers to engage with the *guji* meaning-making through their own poetic responses. This way, its cultural significance and memory-making can continue across time.

Third, this *guji* entry presents a more careful investigation into its historical connection with the nearby temple, so as to further trace the exact location of the site of this house as a *guji*. This confirms that tracing the site of a *guji* and presenting the process of site tracing were deemed important. The result of the site-tracing efforts, however, would not much affect its status as a *guji*. As one can see, the local gazetteer compiler Zheng Yongxi had tried to search for the site, which, however, yielded a result denied by the locals. He chose to report this contradiction to "pass on doubts as doubts" and his engagement in recollecting *gu* (the past).

Through this analysis of the House of Yin Hao, I have illustrated how *guji* as a Chinese discourse of heritage was operated to make meaning of the past in an integrated fashion. Although the physical structure and material remains of the house had long been lost, it continued to be a memorable *guji* for over a thousand years through an intricate interweaving of site tracing, biographical narratives of the historical figure associated, poetic responses to past poem writings, and connection to a local belief. Even in the Republican China era, the local historian still tried to trace its site in the spirit of recollecting *gu*. Regrettably, this site is no longer included in contemporary heritage work, for example, the Third National Survey of Immovable Heritage (Quzhou) in 2009. Why not? The answer is simple: because it has no materiality to authenticate its existence. Perceptibly, for heritage researchers and practitioners today, it is nonsensical that a historic house that had lost its material remains for so long should still be remembered as heritage. However, for the premodern Chinese, this would not be surprising at all because *guji* was not considered to have innate values residing in its materiality. A *guji* was but a dynamic site of past–present interactions, where memory and meaning-making continue to evolve across time. The meaning-making of a *guji* would not stop if there were cultural associations with and remembrance of virtuous historical or divine figures, their deeds and words, as well as different later generations' poetic responses and affective empathies to bridge the past and the present.

As stated in the epigraph, though standing amid the ruins or empty sites, the premodern Chinese could still trace the aura of the past as a source of inspiration for the present and the future. Long before critical heritage researchers, they understood that *guji,* or what we today tend to call heritage, is a process of meaning-making and emotional resonance, rather than an object to be preserved as it was (Macdonald 2013; Onciul 2015; Rico 2021; Smith 2006, 2020). Indeed, as Harvey (2024: 5) states, "Seeing something called 'heritage' as a process [...] is not actually very innovative; people have been doing it for thousands of years." This cultural discourse or alternative idea of heritage in historical China well teaches us that historic preservation is not as much about preserving the old as old, as it is to preserve the cultural modes of rendering the old as meaningful as before. If those cultural modes of meaning-making discontinue, the past or tradition will die.

6 Concluding Remarks

> The Duke of [Ye] informed Confucius, saying, "Among us here, there are those who may be styled upright in their conduct. If their father has stolen a sheep, they will bear witness to the fact." Confucius said, "Among us, in our part of the country, those who are upright are different from this. The father conceals the misconduct of the son, and the son conceals the misconduct of the father. Uprightness is to be found in this."
>
> (Analects 13: 18; Legge's translation with modification 1991: 270)

Despite the numerous critiques of contemporary heritage practices, it is undeniable that we do need heritage, just as we need language and discourse. In this concluding section, I review the major issues addressed in this Element through a philosophical (and sometimes theological) lens, particularly the philosophies of language and history. What I hope is to stimulate further rethinking, inquiries, and debates on heritage while providing summaries of my research findings and viewpoints from a broader perspective.

What is in a Word?

"There is no such thing as heritage" (Smith 2006: 13; Waterton & Smith 2009). This provocative statement might make many upset, if not irritated. Actually, what Smith and Waterton want to argue is that nothing is heritage by nature; things are heritage only when they are so called or recognized by human beings. In other words, heritage gains its existence in and through our speaking of things as heritage. The studies of heritage, therefore, need to pay adequate attention to the language employed to represent and construct, categorize and communicate it.

However, when scholars critique heritage as a form of discursive practice in and through language, many feel upset, at a loss, or even angry. Heritage seems to be driven to nihilism. More than a decade ago, some critical heritage scholars began to indicate that we should not dwell too much on what the discursive turn brings to us but should pay more attention to other important facets of heritage, especially "the ways in which heritage is caught up in the quotidian bodily practices of dwelling, travelling, working and 'being' in the world" (Harrison 2013: 113). The most influential scholar in promoting heritage as discourse, Laurajane Smith, appears to be more interested in emotion than in discourse in recent years. Do we really have enough attention to and work on heritage discourses? No, we do not. For one thing, heritage in our quotidian, bodily practices of dwelling, traveling, working, and being is intertwined with and shaped by language and discourse. Foucault (1978), for instance, has well shown that sexuality – the most intimate bodily practice – is also influenced by discourse. For Heidegger (2001), it is in poetry – a particular genre or mode of language use characterized by its diverse possibilities of interpretation – that we humans can truly dwell and find true being in the world. Therefore, I argue that our studies of heritage (as) discourse are still insufficient. At least, we need more efforts to explore alternative words and discourses to construct and make meaning of "heritage" in various cultural and historical contexts.

In this Element, I have examined a key word analogous to heritage, that is, *guji*, in cultural-historical China. Indeed, if the existence of heritage is only found in words, critical heritage studies should aim not only at deconstructing the universalized terms and ways of speaking, but also, and more importantly, at rearticulating alternative discourses and their underlying ways of meaning-making of the past. As a modern term or concept, *guji* is not distinctive, as it has been transformed by the globalized idea of heritage, particularly tangible heritage, when China began to embrace Western historical consciousness and the ethos of historic conservation over the last hundred years or so. I have traced what this word used to mean and what was articulated about it in a premodern Chinese context, particularly in Quzhou from the 1500s to the 1920s, attempting to disclose it as a forgotten cultural discourse of what we today call "heritage." In doing so, I have demonstrated that heritage could exist differently from how UNESCO, ICOMOS, and national and local heritage institutions define it, and from how archeologists, architects, art historians, and even some critical heritage researchers conceptualize it. *Guji*, as my analysis has unpacked, used to operate under alternative logics of categorizing, meaning-making, and remembering. It was not clearly defined through a standardized system of categorization, opening up its boundaries for negotiation and change. In terms of meaning-making, what was important then was not the physical remains, but those historical (divine) figures, their deeds and words, as well as the emotional bond a site fostered across time. Though materially disappeared, it was still deemed meaningful to trace the site where a *guji* had physically existed and to make the tracing process known to the present and later generations. This well reflects the idea of *ji* in the word *guji*: traces of human steps, but more than the physical vestiges left. What is more, it should be heeded that the concern over materiality or physicality is not simply a yes or no question in the discourse of *guji*. Though it was more often insignificant or out of the process of *guji* meaning-making, one should not simply claim that the Chinese cultural thinking of heritage always excludes any physical or material concerns. As I have shown, when the physical facets, usually the structure and scale, of a *guji* were given attention, another Chinese word,

Li – "the determinate fabric of Chinese culture" (Hall & Ames 1998: 269) – should be crucial. It was through this guiding discourse in traditional China that the meaning of a *guji*'s physical being and the underlying alternative politics of the past were expressed.

Indeed, as heritage is in words and discourses, different words and ways of speaking of heritage can ascribe to it divergent modes of existence. Such divergences should be especially valued and endorsed in the contemporary world. Heritage should be diverse across the world, just like language and discourse should not be homogeneous. In the Christian Bible, God punished human beings when they arrogantly built the Tower of Babel to reach the sky by making them speak different languages (Genesis 11: 1–9). Today, are humans again attempting to achieve excellence of humanity through uniting their language of science, technology, economy, politics, education, culture, and, indeed, heritage?

In this globalized world, cultural diversity is under serious threat. That is a fundamental reason why heritage is needed. Ironically, the idea of heritage itself becomes globalized and homogeneous. In this Element, I have showcased a constructive or "more than critical" (Harvey 2024) approach to deconstruct heritage universalism and homogeneity. It is not about doing critical analysis of the globalized, but about revisiting a forgotten or transformed cultural-historical Other for dialogue. Through this, I hope my readers will not only know better about a forgotten Chinese alternative to heritage, but also be led to imagine how many different alternatives we might have in this vast world in the long passage of time we human beings have gone through. As indicated in the dialogue between Confucius and the Duke of Ye in the epigraph, two different cultural communities might have very different or even contradicting ideas of uprightness. Of crucial importance is that these two senses of uprightness are in dialogue, without a presumption that one is right, and the other is wrong. They coexist to stimulate reflexivity and mutual learning, as I have contended elsewhere (Hou 2020). Readers of this dialogue should ask themselves: Is my (cultural) understanding of uprightness applicable to others (other cultures)? How many different (cultural) understandings of uprightness are there in this world? How might these (cultural) understandings magnify my (culture's) understanding of uprightness? In such reflexive thinking, the cultural diversity of uprightness could be anticipated (144). In the same vein, through revisiting local, cultural discourses of heritage, one expects cross-cultural dialogue, reflexivity, and mutual learning to attain diversity. The Chinese have learned from the West so much and for such a long period of time that they have almost forgotten their cultural discourse of *guji*. They now need to relearn this cultural idea for the diversity of heritage research and practice in China. For other cultures, *guji*, as a Chinese idea of heritage, can be a resource for intercultural learning and an inspiration for them to relearn their own heritage pasts and reshape their own heritage futures.

Uses of Heritage, or Uses of Language

Discussing the use and abuse of history in Europe, Friedrich Nietzsche remarks:

> We need history, certainly, but we need it for reasons different from those for which the idler in the garden of knowledge needs it, even though he may look nobly down on our rough and charmless needs and requirements. We need it, that is to say, for the sake of life and action, not so as to turn comfortably away from life and action, let alone for the purpose of extenuating the self-seeking life and the base and cowardly action. We want to serve history only to the extent that history serves life . . . (Nietzsche 1997: 59)

In today's China and the wider world, we are not only in need of history, but also heritage – an extension of history – and perhaps more urgently than ever before. But how do we need heritage? Do we need it for clearer pictures or more complete knowledge of the past? As critical heritage scholars have pointed out, the construction of heritage as testimony of the past, or as evidence from which the past is known, objectifies it and distances it even further away from us (see, e.g., Lowenthal 1985, 1998). In this way, heritage is dead, like our treatment of history as an object or subject of knowledge. As Nietzsche (1997: 67) observes, "A historical phenomenon, known clearly and completely and resolved into a phenomenon of knowledge, is, for him who has perceived it, dead." How can we, as Nietzsche expects, use history and heritage "only insofar as it serves living?"

Undeniably, heritage is utilized in various locales of China and the wider world to serve certain people's living in economic terms. But for Nietzsche, living as life and action does not mean this. Being "a pupil of earlier times," or a classicist, he wants history to serve our life and action as something untimely, something that disturbs the present. That is, history should be "acting counter to our time and thereby acting on our time and, let us hope, for the benefit of a time to come" (60).

China has a long tradition of classical or historical studies like this. Confucius was a great classicist in this sense. His writing of the *Chunqiu* (*Spring and Autumn Annals*) was intended to act counter to his time and thereby to act on it and expect a time to come. Sima Qian well explicates this by quoting Dong Zhongshu (董仲舒, 179 BCE – 104 BCE), one of the most prominent Confucian scholars in the Han dynasty:

> Sir Hu Sui asked, "For what purposes did Confucius compose the *Chunqiu* in his time?" The grand historian said, "Dong Zhongshu remarks, as I heard

him, '[At his time] the Dao of the Zhou dynasty had fallen into decline. [...] Confucius knew that words would not be used and the Dao would not be practiced. He then righted and wronged what had happened during the 242 years. In doing so, he set the example for the world to follow, critiqued the Son of Heaven, denounced the dukes, and condemned the high officials in order to achieve the career of the sage-kings.'" [上大夫壶遂曰: "昔孔子何为而作春秋哉？" 太史公曰: "余闻董生曰: '周道衰废, [......]。孔子知言之不用, 道之不行也, 是非二百四十二年之中, 以为天下仪表, 贬天子, 退诸侯, 讨大夫, 以达王事而已矣。'"] (Sima 1959: 3297)

Confucius had made himself a pupil of the past about two thousand years earlier than Nietzsche. His renarration of the 242-year history was to counter and critique the ruling elites who did not act in line with the Dao of Zhou, including the Tianzi (Son of Heaven) or the king, the dukes and the high officials. As such, he was a genuine classicist acting on his time and hoping for a time to come (back). A key strategy in this Confucian tradition of history-making, I would like to stress, is the reuse of authentic language from the past, as *gu* was considered integral to the language passed down from earlier generations. Confucius, a transmitter of *gu* (Analects 7: 1; Legge 1991: 195), as he claimed, worked hard to pass down the Dao and the language in which it is embedded. For him, the Dao is with the language from the past, and the problems in the present are usually attributed to the discontinued correct reuse of ancient words, particularly those of the sage-kings (see Wu 2014b).

This Chinese tradition in transmitting words of the past, especially words of respectful and virtuous historical figures, has been fundamentally important for the Chinese in their *guji* making. As my discourse analysis in this volume has displayed, the language from the past, especially that by respectful local and national historical figures of poetic quality, and the stories about them are greatly valued in the meaning-making of a *guji*. Such meaning-making of the past in words and narratives transmitted from the past was not for the sake of knowledge but in hoping to use the past language to address the present, often in order to counteract the present in moral and political terms. *Guji* was considered a resource for *guan* and *xing* to call for respectful emotions, ethical actions, and the observance of *Li*. It was expected to make people venerate the past, especially the virtuous historical figures from whom they could learn how to live like a *junzi* (君子), and to warn people not to act in ways that violate the rules of *Li*.

As such, *guji* can also add some insights to the debates around heritage ethics (Colwell & Joy 2015; Ireland & Schofield 2015; Meskell 2010; Rico 2017), urging us to consider the ethical use of heritage or the use of heritage for ethical purposes. This is a pressing issue in China and the wider world, as people from different walks of life are worrying about the moral deterioration in our societies. Can our heritage be utilized for the humility of ourselves? Can we allow heritage to turn us into pupils of the past? Can heritage help us live as ethically pleasing beings? I hope this volume on *guji* as a Chinese discourse of heritage can also stimulate more intercultural debates on the ethics of heritage from diverse approaches, rather than being confined to ownership, rights and identity. After all, is it ethically unpleasant if heritage ethics focuses merely on claiming and reclaiming properties, rights, and identities? If heritage exists in language and discourse, who really owns it? Who can claim rights for it? And who cannot find identification with the associated historical figures if they are able to understand the language?

References

Adams, J. (2013). The role of underwater archaeology in framing and facilitating the Chinese national strategic agenda. In T. Blumenfield & H. Silverman (Eds.), *Cultural heritage politics in China* (pp. 261–282). New York: Springer.

Akagawa, N. (2016). Rethinking the global heritage discourse – overcoming "East" and "West"? *International Journal of Heritage Studies*, 22(1), 14–25.

Angouri, J., Paraskevaidi, M., & Wodak, R. (2017). Discourses of cultural heritage in times of crisis: The case of the Parthenon Marbles. *Journal of Sociolinguistics*, 21(2), 208–237.

Astudillo, A. E., & Salazar, N. B. (2024). Heritage imaginaries and imaginaries of heritage: An analytical lens to rethink heritage from 'alter-native' ontologies. *International Journal of Heritage Studies*, 30(2), 181–194.

Azaryahu, M. (2021). *An everlasting name: Cultural remembrance and traditions of onymic commemoration*. Berlin: Walter de Gruyter.

Barry, R., & Teron, L. (2023). Visualising heritage: A critical discourse analysis of place, race, and nationhood along the Erie Canal. *Local Environment*, 28(6), 739–752.

Basso, K. (1996). Wisdom sits in places: Landscape and language among the Western Apache. In Feld, S. and K. Basso (Eds.), *Senses of place* (pp. 51–90) Santa Fe, NM: School of American Research Press.

Bi, L., Vanneste, D., & van der Borg, J. (2016). Cultural heritage development in China: A contextualized trajectory or a global-local nexus? *International Journal of Cultural Property*, 23(2), 191–207.

Bloembergen, M., & Eickhoff, M. (2020). *The politics of heritage in Indonesia: A cultural history*. Cambridge: Cambridge University Press.

Blommaert, J. (2005). *Discourse: A critical introduction*. Cambridge: Cambridge University Press.

Blumenfield, T., & Silverman, H. (Eds.) (2013). *Cultural heritage politics in China*. New York: Springer.

Brown, S. (2023). From culture and nature as separate to interconnected naturecultures. In S. Brown & C. Goetcheus (Eds.), *Routledge handbook of cultural landscape practice* (pp. 47–61). New York: Routledge.

Byrne, D. (1991). Western hegemony in archaeological heritage management. *History and Anthropology*, 5(2), 269–276.

Byrne, D. (2014). *Counterheritage: Critical perspectives on heritage conservation in Asia*. Abingdon: Routledge.

Cang, X. L. (1990). 方志学通论 [*A general treatise on local gazetteer studies*]. Jinan: Qilu Shushe.

Carbaugh, D. (1996). *Situating selves: The communication of social identities in American scenes*. New York: SUNY Press.

Carbaugh, D. (2007). Cultural discourse analysis: Communication practices and intercultural encounters. *Journal of Intercultural Communication Research*, 36(3), 167–182.

Chan, S. (2012). Cosmology, society, and humanity: *Tian* in the *Guodian* texts (part II). *Journal of Chinese Philosophy*, 39(1), 106–120.

Chard, R. L. (2011). Perspectives on "li" and "ritual" in Western Sinology. *World Sinology*, (Autumn), 29–37.

Chen, P. (Supervised), Xu, Z. et al. (Compiled). (1699). 西安县志 [Xi'an county gazetteer]. The Kangxi 38th year engraved edition.

Cheng, C.-Y. (2003). Dao (tao): The Way. In Antonio Cua (Ed.), *Encyclopedia of Chinese philosophy* (pp. 202–206). London: Routledge.

Cheng, C.-Y. (2008). The Yi-Jing and Yin-Yang way of thinking. In Z. Mou (Ed.), *The Routledge history of Chinese philosophy* (pp. 71–106). London: Routledge.

Cheng, T. W. (1999). Preface. In Yao, C. X. 吴越访古录 [Records of visiting the past in the Wu and Yue regions]. Nanjing: Jiangsu Guji Chunbanshe.

Chung, S.-J. (2005). East Asian values in historic conservation. *Journal of Architectural Conservation*, 11(1), 55–70.

Colwell, C., & Joy, C. (2015). Communities and ethics in the heritage debates. In L. Meskell (Ed.), *Global heritage: A reader* (pp. 112–130). Oxford: Wiley-Blackwell.

Coupland, B., & Coupland, N. (2014). The authenticating discourses of mining heritage tourism in Cornwall and Wales. *Journal of Sociolinguistics*, 18(4), 495–517.

Coupland, N., Garrett, P., & Bishop, H. (2005). Wales underground: Discursive frames and authenticities in Welsh mining heritage tourism events. In A. Jaworski & A. Prichard (Eds.), *Discourse, communication and tourism* (pp. 191–221). Bristol: Channel View Publications.

D'Agostino, S. (2021). *Conservation and restoration of built heritage: A history of conservation culture and its more recent developments*. Leiden: CRC Press.

De Cesari, C. (2019). *Heritage and the cultural struggle for Palestine*. Stanford, CA: Stanford University Press.

De Jong, F., & Rowlands, M. (Eds.). (2007). *Reclaiming heritage: Alternative imaginaries of memory in West Africa*. Walnut Creek, CA: Left Coast Press.

Eriksen, A. (2014). *From antiquities to heritage: Transformations of cultural memory*. New York: Berghahn Books.

Evans, H., & Rowlands, M. (2021). *Grassroots values and local cultural heritage in China*. Lanham, MD: Lexington Books.

Evers, S., & Seagle, C. (2012). Stealing the sacred: Why "global heritage" discourse is perceived as a frontal attack on local heritage-making in Madagascar. *Madagascar Conservation & Development* 7(2S): 97–106.

Fairclough, N. (1992). *Discourse and social change*. Cambridge: Polity Press.

Falser, M. (2020). *Angkor Wat: A transcultural history of heritage (Vols. I and II)*. Berlin: De Gruyter.

Fang, T. (2012). Yin Yang: A new perspective on culture. *Management and Organization Review*, 8(1), 25–50.

Fang, X. et al. (1974). 晋书 (第七册) [The book of Jin (Vol. 7)]. Beijing: Zhonghua Shuju.

Feng, J., Dai, L., Jiang, J., & Wei, R. (2018). A matter of perspective: A discursive analysis of the perceptions of three stakeholders of the Mutianyu Great Wall. *IEEE Transactions on Professional Communication*, 61(1), 22–47.

Feng, J., Li, Y., & Wu, P. (2017). Conflicting images of the Great Wall in cultural heritage tourism. *Critical Arts*, 31(6), 109–127.

Flowerdew, J. (2012). *Critical discourse analysis in historiography: The case of Hong Kong's evolving identity*. Basingstoke: Palgrave Macmillan.

Foucault, M. (1972). *The archaeology of knowledge* (A. M. Sheridan, trans.). London: Tavistock Publications.

Foucault, M. (1977). *Discipline and punish: The birth of the prison*. London: Allen Lane.

Foucault, M. (1978). *The history of sexuality. Volume 1: An introduction*. New York: Random House.

Foucault, M. (1984). Nietzsche, genealogy, history. In P. Rabinow (Ed.), *The Foucault reader* (pp. 76–100). New York: Pantheon Books.

Foucault, M. (1989). *The order of things: An archaeology of the human sciences*. London: Routledge.

Gao, Q., & Jones, S. (2021). Authenticity and heritage conservation: Seeking common complexities beyond the "Eastern" and "Western" dichotomy. *International Journal of Heritage Studies*, 27(1), 90–106.

Gillman, D. (2010). *The idea of cultural heritage (Revised edition)*. Cambridge: Cambridge University Press.

Gosden, C., & Marshall, Y. (1999). The cultural biography of objects. *World Archaeology* 31(2), 169–178.

Graham, A. C. (1986). *Yin-Yang and the nature of correlative thinking* (Vol. 6). Singapore: Institute of East Asian Philosophies.

Hall, D. L., & Ames, R. T. (1998). *Thinking from the Han: Self, truth, and transcendence in Chinese and Western culture*. Albany: SUNY Press.

Hall, S. (1999). Whose heritage? Un-settling "the heritage", re-imagining the post-nation. *Third Text*, 13(49), 3–13.

Hao, Y. (Supervised), Lu, Z. et al. (Compiled). (1730). 广东通志 [Guangdong Provincial Gazetteer]. Wenyuange Complete Library in the Four Branches of Literature version.

Harrison, R. (Ed.). (2010). *Understanding the politics of heritage*. Manchester: Manchester University Press.

Harrison, R. (2013). *Heritage: Critical approaches*. London: Routledge.

Harrison, R. (2015). Beyond "natural" and "cultural" heritage: Toward an ontological politics of heritage in the age of Anthropocene. *Heritage & Society*, 8(1), 24–42.

Harvey, D. C. (2001). Heritage pasts and heritage presents: Temporality, meaning and the scope of heritage studies. *International Journal of Heritage Studies*, 7(4), 319–338.

Harvey, D. C. (2024). What's in a word? Reflections on, challenges to, and possibilities with the ACHS. *International Journal of Heritage Studies*, 30(12), 1496–1501.

Heidegger, M. (2001). The poet as thinker. In A. Hofstadter (trans. & ed.), *Poetry, language, thought* (pp. 1–14). New York: Perennial Classics.

Hou, S. (2019). Remembering trees as heritage: *Guji* discourse and the meaning-making of trees in Hangzhou, Qing China, *International Journal of Heritage Studies*, 25(5): 455–468.

Hou, S. (2020). From meaning seeking to dialogue and reflexivity: A textual-discursive interpretation of "mutual concealment among family members" in the Analects. *Universitas-Monthly Review of Philosophy and Culture*, 47(1), 133–148.

Hou, S., Liu, H., & Gac, J. (2019). 语言原真性与文化遗产的意义生成——以浙江衢州"周王庙"为中心的考察 [Language authenticity and the meaning-making of Chinese cultural heritage: A narrative (re)construction of the Zhouwang Temple in Quzhou, Zhejiang], *Southeast Culture* (5), 6–13.

Hou, S., & Wu, Z. (2012). 话语分析与文化遗产的本土意义解读——以衢州方志中的"文昌殿"为例 [Discourse analysis and the interpretation of indigenous meanings of Chinese cultural heritage: A case study of the Wenchang Palace], *Southeast Culture* (4), 21–27.

Hou, S., & Wu, Z. (2015). 历史话语何以有用?——从文化遗产探索批评话语分析的文化路径 [How are past discourses useful to the present? From cultural heritage to a cultural approach to critical discourse analysis], *Foreign Language Research* (3), 47–52.

Hou, S., & Wu, Z. (2017). Writing multi-discursive ethnography as critical discourse study: The case of the Wenchang Palace in Quzhou, China. *Critical Discourse Studies*, 14(1), 73–89.

Hou, S., Wu, Z., & Liu, H. (2016). Multi-discursive ethnography and the re-narration of Chinese heritage: Stories about the *Yueju* opera performance at the Heavenly Queen Palace of Quzhou. *Sungkyun Journal of East Asian Studies*, 16(2), 197–222.

Huang, C. (1997). 中国近代史学的双重危机: 试论"新史学"的诞生及其所面临的困境 [The dual crisis of modern Chinese historiography: A discussion on the birth of "new historiography" and the predicaments it faced]. *Journal of the Institute of Chinese Culture*, 6, 263–285.

Ireland, T. & Schofield, J. (Eds). (2015). *The ethics of cultural heritage*. New York: Springer.

James, L., & Winter, T. (2017). Expertise and the making of world heritage policy. *International Journal of Cultural Policy*, 23(1), 36–51.

Jokilehto, J. (2017). *A history of architectural conservation* (2nd edition). Abingdon: Routledge.

Katelieva, M., Muhar, A., & Penker, M. (2020). Nature-related knowledge as intangible cultural heritage: Safeguarding and tourism utilisation in Austria. *Journal of Tourism and Cultural Change*, 18(6), 673–689.

Kearney, A. (2009). Homeland emotion: An emotional geography of heritage and homeland. *International Journal of Heritage Studies*, 15(2–3), 209–222.

Lai, G. L. (2016). The emergence of "cultural heritage" in modern China: A historical and legal perspective. In A. Matsuda & L. E. Mengoni (Eds.), *Reconsidering cultural heritage in East Asia* (pp. 47–85). London: Ubiquity Press.

Lai, G. L., M. Demas, & N. Agnew (2004). Valuing the past in China: the seminal influence of Liang Sicheng on heritage conservation. *Orientations*, 35(2): 82–89.

Legge, J. (Trans.). (1885). *Li Ki: The book of rites*. In *The sacred books of the East* (Vols. 27 & 28). Oxford: Clarendon Press.

Legge, J. (Trans.) (1876). *The She King, or, The book of ancient poetry*. London: Trübner.

Legge, J. (Trans.). (1991). Confucius Analects. In *The Chinese Classics* (pp. 137–354). Taipei: SMC Publishing.

Li, C. (2013). 由名胜古迹谈遗产的中国范式 [Discussing the Chinese paradigm of heritage from the perspective of famous historical sites: Taking "The

Middle of Heaven and Earth" as an example]. *Guizhou Social Sciences* (4), 16–21.

Li, J. (2005). 什么是文化遗产？对一个当代观念的知识考古 [What is cultural heritage? An archaeology of knowledge approach to a contemporary concept]. *Literature & Art Studies* (4): 123–131.

Li, M. (2020). Looking back to quiddity between traditional Chinese architecture and ancestor worship. *Journal of Chinese Architecture and Urbanism*, 2(1), 1–14.

Lin, Y. T. (1937). *The importance of living*. New York: Reynal & Hitchcock.

Lin, Y. (Supervised), Ye, B. et al. (2009). 天启衢州府志 [Tianqi Quzhou prefectural gazetteer]. In Quzhou Municipal Office of Local Gazetteers (Eds.). 衢州府志集成 [A Collection of Quzhou prefectural gazetteers] (pp. 351–610). Hangzhou: Xilingyinshe Chubanshe.

Littler, J., & Naidoo, R. (Eds.). (2005). *The politics of heritage: The legacies of race*. London: Routledge.

Liu, L. H. (1995). *Translingual practice: Literature, national culture, and translated modernity – China, 1900–1937*. Stanford, CA: Stanford University Press.

Losson, P. (2022). *The return of cultural heritage to Latin America: Nationalism, policy, and politics in Colombia, Mexico, and Peru*. London: Routledge.

Lowenthal, D. (1989). Material preservation and its alternatives. *Perspecta*, 25, 67–77.

Lowenthal, D. (1998). *The heritage crusade and the spoils of history (second edition)*. New York: Cambridge University Press.

Lu, X. (1973). 伪自由书 [A letter of fake freedom]. In the Commemoration Committee of Mr. Lu Xun (Eds.) 鲁迅全集 (第五卷) [*A complete collection of Lu Xun (Vol.5)*] (pp. 1–196). Beijing: Renmin Wenxue Chubanshe.

Macdonald, S. (2013). *Memorylands: Heritage and identity in Europe today*. Abingdon: Routledge.

Marchant, A. (Ed.). (2019). *Historicising heritage and emotions: The affective histories of blood, stone and land*. Abingdon: Routledge.

Melis, C., & Chambers, D. (2021). The construction of intangible cultural heritage: A Foucauldian critique. *Annals of Tourism Research*, 89, 103206.

Meskell, L. (2010). Human rights and heritage ethics. *Anthropological Quarterly*, 83(4), 839–859.

Meskell, L. (2021). *Object worlds in ancient Egypt: Material biographies past and present*. New York: Routledge.

Mote, F. W. (1973). *A millennium of Chinese urban history: Form, time, and space concepts in Soochow* (Rice Institute Pamphlet – Rice University Studies, 59). Houston: Rice University.

Nietzsche, F. (1997). On the uses and disadvantages of history for life. In D. Breazeale (Ed.), *Untimely meditations* (R. J. Hollingdale, trans., pp. 57–123). Cambridge: Cambridge University Press.

Nikkilä, P. (1992). T'ien, Heaven. *Studia Orientalia Electronica*, 68, 20–49.

Nora, P. (1989). Between memory and history: *Les lieux de mémoire*. *Representations*, 26, 7–24.

Novoa, M. (2023). Gendered nostalgia: Grassroots heritage tourism and (de)industrialization in Lota, Chile. *Journal of Heritage Tourism*, 18(3), 365–383.

Onciul, B. (2015). *Museums, heritage and indigenous voice: Decolonizing engagement*. Abingdon: Routledge.

Pastor Pérez, A., & Colomer, L. (2024). Dissecting authorised participation in cultural heritage. *International Journal of Heritage Studies*, 30(2), 226–241.

Peng, Z. (2018). 生生遗续、代代相承——中国非物质文化遗产体系研究[*The continuity through lives and inheritance across generations: Exploring China's intangible cultural heritage system*]. Beijing: Peking University Press.

Reisigl, M., & Wodak, R. (2015). The discourse-historical approach (DHA). In R. Wodak & M. Meyer (Eds.), *Methods of critical discourse studies* (3rd ed., pp. 23–61). Sage.

Rico, T. (2016). *Constructing destruction: Heritage narratives in the tsunami city*. New York: Routledge.

Rico, T. (2017). Expertise and heritage ethics in the Middle East. *International Journal of Middle East Studies*, 49, 742–746.

Rico, T. (2021). *Global heritage, religion, and secularism*. Cambridge University Press.

Ruan, Y. & Lin, L. (2003). 文化遗产保护的原真性原则 [Authenticity in relation to the conservation of cultural heritage]. *Tongji University Journal (Social Science Section)* (2), 1–5.

Ryckmans, P. (1986). *The Chinese attitude towards the past*, Forty-seventh George Ernest Morrison Lecture on Ethnology. Canberra: Australian National University. https://openresearch-repository.anu.edu.au/bitstream/1885/145845/2/Morrison%20Oration%2047.pdf.

Schmidt, P. (2010). Trauma and social memory in Northwestern Tanzania: Organic, spontaneous community collaboration. *Journal of Social Archaeology*, 10(2), 255–279.

Schmidt, P. (2017). *Community-based heritage in Africa: Unveiling local research and development initiatives*. New York: Routledge.

Shen, J. (Supervised), Wu X. et al. (Complied) (2009). 弘治衢州府志 [Hongzhi Quzhou prefectural gazetteer]. In Quzhou Municipal Office of Local Gazetteers (Ed.), *A collection of Quzhou prefectural gazetteers* [衢州府志集成] (pp. 1–128). Hangzhou: Xilingyinshe Chubanshe.

Sheng, S. (1747). 仪礼集编 [*A collection of Yili commentaries*], Wenyuange Complete Library in the Four Branches of Literature version.

Shepherd, R., & Yu, L. (2013). *Heritage management, tourism, and governance in China: Managing the past to serve the present*. New York: Springer.

Shi-xu. (2005). *A cultural approach to discourse*. Basingstoke: Palgrave Macmillan.

Shi-xu. (2012). *Why do cultural discourse studies? Towards a culturally conscious and critical approach to human discourses*. Critical Arts, 26(4), 484–503.

Shi-xu. (2014). *Chinese discourse studies*. Basingstoke: Palgrave Macmillan.

Shi-xu. (2015). Cultural discourse studies. In K. Tracy, C. Ilie, & T. Sandel (Eds.), The *International Encyclopedia of Language and Social Interaction* (pp. 1–9). Oxford: John Wiley & Sons.

Sima, Qian. (1959). *Shiji* 史记 (第十册) [*The records of the Grand Historian (vol. 10)*]. Beijing: Zhonghua shuju.

Skrede, J. (2020). Discourse analysis and non-representational theories in heritage studies: A non-reductionist take on their compatibility. *Journal of Cultural Geography*, 37(1), 88–108.

Skrede, J., & Andersen, B. (2023). Visualising the past for the future: A social semiotic reading of urban heritage. *Social Semiotics*, 33(5), 1147–1164.

Skrede, J., & Hølleland, H. (2018). Uses of heritage and beyond: Heritage studies viewed through the lens of critical discourse analysis and critical realism. *Journal of Social Archaeology*, 18(1), 77–96.

Smith, L. (2004). *Archaeological theory and the politics of cultural heritage*. London: Routledge.

Smith, L. (2006). *Uses of heritage*. London: Routledge.

Smith, L. (2011). Heritage and its intangibility. In A. Skounti et O. Tebbaa (Eds.), *De l'immatérialité du patrimoine culturel* (pp. 10–20). Marrakech: Bureau régional de l'unesco de Rabat.

Smith, L. (2020). *Emotional heritage: Visitor engagement at museums and heritage sites*. Abingdon: Routledge.

Smith, L., & Campbell, G. (2016). The elephant in the room: Heritage, affect, and emotion. In W. Logan, M. N. C. Máiréad, & U. Kockel (Eds.),

A companion to heritage studies (pp. 443–460). Chichester: Wiley-Blackwell.

Smith, L., Wetherell, M., & Campbell, G. (Eds.). (2018). *Emotion, affective practices, and the past in the present*. Abingdon: Routledge.

Su, X., & Teo, P. (2009). *The politics of heritage tourism in China: A view from Lijiang*. London: Routledge.

Sundin, B. (2005). Nature as heritage: The Swedish case. *International Journal of Heritage Studies*, 11(1), 9–20.

Svensson, M., & Maags, C. (2018). *Chinese heritage in the making: Experiences, negotiations and contestations*. Amsterdam: Amsterdam University Press.

Swenson, A. (2013). *The rise of heritage: Preserving the past in France, Germany and England, 1789–1914*. Cambridge: Cambridge University Press.

Taylor, J. (2015). Embodiment unbound: Moving beyond divisions in the understanding and practice of heritage conservation. *Studies in Conservation*, 60(1), 65–77.

Tang, M. (2015). 论民国《衢县志》的文本特色与价值 [On the textual features and values of the Qu County Gazetteer]. *Zhejiang Academic Journal* (2), 95–102.

Tian, K. (2012). 清代成都官署的建设 [Reconstruction of Chengdu's government offices in Qing dynasty]. *Journal of Southwest Jiaotong University (Social Sciences Edition)* (5), 103–109.

Tian, W., Wang, S. et al. (Supervised), Sun, H., Gu, D. et al. (Compiled). (1735). 河南通志 [*He'nan provincial gazetteer*]. Wenyuange Complete Library in the Four Branches of Literature version.

Tolia-Kelly, D. P., Waterton, E., & Watson, S. (Eds.) (2017). *Heritage, affect and emotion. Politics, practices and infrastructures*. Abingdon: Routledge.

Tuan, Y.-F. (1991). Language and the making of place: A narrative-descriptive approach. *Annals of the Association of American Geographers*, 81(4), 684–696.

UNESCO. (1972). *Convention concerning the protection of the world cultural and natural Heritage*. Paris: United Nations Educational, Scientific and Cultural Organization. https://whc.unesco.org/archive/convention-en.pdf.

Walsh, K. (1992). *The representation of the past: Museums and heritage in the post-modern world*. London: Routledge.

Wang, D. (2020). *Longmen's stone buddhas and cultural heritage: When antiquity met modernity in China*. Lanham, MD: Rowman & Littlefield.

Wang, Q. E. (2001). *Inventing China through history: The May Fourth approach to historiography*. Albany: State University of New York Press.

Wang, S. L. (2017). Exhibiting the nation: Cultural flows, transnational exchanges and the development of museums in Japan and China in the early twentieth century. In C. Stolte & Y. Kikuchi (Eds.), *Eurasian encounters: Museums, missions and modernities* (pp. 47–72). Amsterdam: Amsterdam University Press.

Wang, S. L., & Rowlands, M. (2017). Making and unmaking heritage values in China. In H. Geismar & J. Anderson (Eds.), *The Routledge companion to cultural property* (pp. 258–274). Abingdon: Routledge.

Wang, Y. E. (2003). Tope and topos: The Leifeng Pagoda and the discourse of the demonic. In J. Zeitlin & L. Liu (Eds.), *Writing and materiality in China* (pp. 488–552). Cambridge, MA: Harvard University Press.

Wang, Y. L. (2009), 中国文物保护单位制度研究 [A study of *Chinese Wenwu Baohu* policies]. PhD diss., Fudan University.

Waterton, E. (2009). Sights of sites: Picturing heritage, power and exclusion. *Journal of Heritage Tourism*, 4(1), 37–56.

Waterton, E. (2010a). *Politics, policy and the discourses of heritage in Britain*. Basingstoke: Palgrave Macmillan.

Waterton, E. (2010b). Branding the past: The visual imagery of England's heritage. In E. Waterton & S. Watson (Eds.), *Culture, heritage and representations: Perspectives on visuality and the past*. Aldershot: Ashgate Publishing.

Waterton, E., & Smith, L., (2009). There is no such thing as heritage. In E. Waterton & L. Smith (Eds.), *Taking archaeology out of heritage* (pp. 10–27). Newcastle-upon-Tyne, UK: Cambridge Scholars Press.

Waterton, E., Smith, L., & Campbell, G. (2006). The utility of discourse analysis to heritage studies: The Burra Charter and social inclusion. *International Journal of Heritage Studies*, 12(4), 339–355.

White, H. (1973). *Metahistory: The historical imagination in 19th-century Europe*. Baltimore: Johns Hopkins University Press.

White, H. (1987). The value of narrativity in the representation of reality. In *The content of the form: Narrative discourse and historical representation* (pp. 1–25). Baltimore: Johns Hopkins University Press.

Wight, A. C. (2016). Lithuanian genocide heritage as discursive formation. *Annals of Tourism Research*, 59, 60–78.

Winter, T. (2014). Beyond Eurocentrism? Heritage conservation and the politics of difference. *International Journal of Heritage Studies*, 20(2), 123–137.

Wu, Z. (2012a). 重建坊巷文化肌理：衢州水亭门街区文化遗产研究 [Reweaving cultural fabrics of neighborhood heritage: The case of Shuitingmen Street cultural heritage study]. *Studies in Culture & Art*, (3), 19–27.

Wu, Z. (2012b). 话语与文化遗产的本土意义建构 [Recovering indigenous discourse of cultural heritage: A Chinese challenge to Western values of heritage]. *Journal of Zhejiang University (Humanities and Social Sciences)*, 42(5), 28–40.

Wu, Z. (2014a). "Speak in the place of the sages": Rethinking the sources of pedagogic meanings. *Journal of Curriculum Studies*, 43(3), 320–331.

Wu, Z. (2014b). Let fragments speak for themselves: Vernacular heritage, emptiness and Confucian discourse of narrating the past. *International Journal of Heritage Studies*, 20(7–8), 851–865.

Wu, Z., & Hou, S. (2015). Heritage and discourse. In E. Waterton & S. Watson (Eds.), *The Palgrave companion to contemporary heritage research* (pp. 37–51). Basingstoke: Palgrave Macmillan.

Wu, Z., & Yao, Y. (2014). 周道对大运河的启示: 本土遗产话语的道统源流 [The implication of Zhou Dao to the search of meanings of the Grand Canal: Confucian orthodoxy of Chinese cultural heritage]. *Journal of Zhejiang University (Humanities and Social Sciences)* (5), 50–62.

Xie, N. (1991). 中国山水文化源流初探 [The origin of Chinese *shanshui* (landscape) culture]. *Chinese Landscape Architecture*, (4): 15–19.

Xu, S. (Compiled), Duan Y. (Commented). (1981). *Commentaries on Shuowen Jiezi* [说文解字注]. Shanghai: Shanghai Guji Chubanshe.

Xu, S. Z. (1998). 文体明辩序说 [*Exploration and elucidation on genres*]. Beijing: Renmin Wenxue Chubanshe.

Yan, H. (2018). *World heritage craze in China: Universal discourse, national culture, and local memory.* Oxford: Berghahn Books.

Yang, J. (1999). 中国方志学概论 [A general introduction to Chinese local gazetteer studies]. Guiyang: Guizhou Renmin Chubanshe.

Yang, T. et al. (Supervised & Compiled). (2009). 康熙衢州府志 [Kangxi Quzhou prefectural gazetteer]. In Quzhou Municipal Office of Local Gazetteers (Eds.), 衢州府志集成 [*A collection of Quzhou prefectural gazetteers*] (pp. 611–1080). Hangzhou: Xilingyinshe Chubanshe.

Yang, Z. (Supervised), Zhao, T. et al. (Compiled). (2009). 嘉靖衢州府志 [Jiajing Quzhou prefectural gazetteer]. In Quzhou Municipal Office of Local Gazetteers (Eds.), 衢州府志集成[*A collection of Quzhou prefectural gazetteers*] (pp. 129–350). Hangzhou: Xilingyinshe Chubanshe.

Yao, B. (Supervised), Fan, C. et al. (Compiled). (1970). 西安县志 [Xi'an county gazetteer]. Taipei: Chengwu chubanshe.

Yu, H., & Mei, J. (2024). Dance improvisation as an embodied encounter with a heritage site: A case in the archaeological ruins of *Liangzhu*. *International Journal of Heritage Studies*, 30(5), 597–611.

Yu, X. (2008). 中国古代遗产保护实践述略 [A survey of heritage protection in ancient China], *Central China Architecture* (3), 1–6.

Yu, X. (2012). 中国古代遗产保护传统制度研究 [A study of the traditional system of heritage preservation in ancient China]. *Journal of Southeast University (Philosophy and Social Sciences Edition)* (1),117–122.

Zhang, C. (2019). 因时随事:遗产实践话语建构的中国范式 [Changing with the time: A Chinese paradigm to the discursive construction of heritage practice]. Hangzhou: Zhejiang University Press.

Zhang, S. (2018). The heritage practices in a Chinese historic neighbourhood: The manifestation of traditional *Feng Shui* in Langzhong, China. *International Journal of Heritage Studies*, 24(5), 531–546.

Zhang, S. J. (2011). 礼经建筑空间的政治叙事 [The politics of narrating architecture space in the *Li* classics]. *Jiangxi Social Sciences* (1), 37–47.

Zhang, R. (2020). *Chinese heritage sites and their audiences: the power of the past*. Abingdon: Routledge.

Zhang, T. Y. et al. (1974). 明史 (第二十四册) [The history of Ming (Vol. 24)]. Beijing: Zhonghua Shuju.

Zhang, Y. S. et al. (2002). 康熙字典 [The Kangxi dictionary]. Shanghai: Hanyu Dacidian Chubanshe.

Zhao, E. X. et al. (1976). 清史稿 [A draft history of Qing]. Beijing: Zhonghua Shuju.

Zhao, H. (Supervised), Huang, Z. (Compiled). (1736). 江南通志 [Jiangnan regional gazetteer]. Wenyuange Complete Library in the Four Branches of Literature version.

Zheng, Y. (1984). 衢县志 [Qu county gazetteer]. Taipei: Chengwu chubanshe.

Zhu, Y. (2015). Cultural effects of authenticity: Contested heritage practices in China. *International Journal of Heritage Studies*, 21(6), 594–608.

Zhu, Y., & Maags, C. (2020). *Heritage politics in China: The power of the past*. Abingdon: Routledge.

Zhu, Y. (2024a). *China's heritage through history: Reconfigured pasts*. New York: Routledge.

Zhu, Y. (2024b). Putting the "critical" in heritage studies from non-Anglophone regions: China and beyond. *International Journal of Heritage Studies*, 30(12), 1476–1486.

Acknowledgments

Some six years ago, a much fuller version of this Element was submitted to a prestigious European publisher. The anonymous reviewer faulted it for not addressing the important issue of heritage politics in China and suggested a rejection of my manuscript. I understand that most critical heritage scholars, at least at that time, did not care much about alternative heritage discourses in historical times but were obsessed with contemporary politics of heritage. They want to explicate how governments and institutions in different parts of the world use heritage for ideological and economic purposes, and how experts and their expertise work in this process as knowledge/power. That is not a problem, but virtually a fashion in critical heritage studies. However, is it not the case that scholarship should strive to counter rather than follow fashions? Should not a reviewer assess a scholarly work based on the importance of the issue addressed and how well it is addressed, rather than the importance, if not popularity, of the issue not explicitly addressed? Actually, my work does take Chinese heritage politics into consideration, though in rather implicit ways. My inquiry into a forgotten alternative for what we now call "heritage" points to the politics of the heritage movement in contemporary China (and the wider world) with a critical edge. As many researchers have pointed out and showcased in this Element, there are divergent ways of doing critical scholarship, and people need "more-than-critical" (Harvey 2024) scholarship. This premise is valid not only in heritage studies but also in other fields of the humanities and social sciences.

Fortunately, as critical heritage studies grow increasingly diverse in recent years, I could more easily find open minds to welcome a critical or, rather, more-than-critical contribution like this one. I would like to record my deepest gratitude to the series editor I had been working with, Professor Michael Rowlands, who, very sadly, passed away from cancer before the publication of this Element. This is a profound loss for us all in the field of heritage studies. He was such an astute intellectual and compassionate person. I was truly thankful for his patience and encouragement in the process, though the deadline of submission was postponed twice for my reasons. I was particularly moved by his commitment to this project even in the last months of his life. In April 2025, he urged me in one of our email exchanges to expedite revisions and language editing in response to reviewer comments, to ensure a timely publication. When I submitted the revised manuscript in June, his silence was uncharacteristic. Two months later, I learned the devastating news of his death from Professor

Kristian Kristiansen, to whom I am immensely grateful for her generosity in carrying this project forward.

My obligations to Professor Xiaoye You at Pennsylvania State University and to the two anonymous reviewers are equally weighty. Their careful readings and constructive comments on earlier drafts proved invaluable in enhancing both the clarity and the rigor of this work. Their insights have also helped me situate this study more effectively within broader scholarly conversations.

During the long process of research, writing, and rewriting, I have been indebted to many scholars I have worked with and talked to. My sincere thanks go to Professor Zongjie Wu, whose unique way of thinking and insightful supervision in the early stage of my research work have fundamentally shaped how I understand heritage, discourse, and critical scholarship. Professor Peter Schmidt's teaching and supervision were also profoundly significant in the emerging stage of this work. To him, my obligations always endure. I am also enormously obliged to Professor Zhaohui Liu, Professor Huimei Liu, Professor Meixin Hu, Dr. Hua Yu, Dr. Chunyan Han, Dr. Yingchun Zhang, Dr. Cuijun Xia, Dr. Yuanyuan Yao, Dr. Yujie Zhu, Professor Guolong Lai, and many others whose names I cannot exhaust here. Their help, advice, and encouragement at various stages were instrumental in bringing my research to fruition.

Section 2 of this Element was revised and developed from the third section of a paper I coauthored in Chinese, namely, Hou, S., & Wu, Z. (2012). *Guji* and cross-cultural interpretations of heritage politics ["古迹"与遗产政治的跨文化解读], *Studies in Culture and Arts* [文化艺术研究] (1), 1–8. I am truly grateful to Professor Wu for consenting to my rewriting it for this Element, and to the journal for permitting its reuse.

Above all, I owe an immeasurable debt to my wife, Dr. Binfang Wu, whose unwavering love and support not only render this book possible, but also make my career and life a lot more meaningful.

Cambridge Elements =

Critical Heritage Studies

Kristian Kristiansen
University of Gothenburg

Michael Rowlands
UCL

About the Series
This series focuses on the recent v established field of Critical Heritage Studies. Interdisciplinary in character, it brings together contributions from experts working in a range of fields, including cultural management, anthropology, archaeology, politics, and law. The series will include volumes that demonstrate the impact of contemporary theoretical discourses on heritage found throughout the world, raising awareness of the acute relevance of critically analysing and understanding the way heritage is used today to form new futures.

Cambridge Elements

Critical Heritage Studies

Elements in the Series

Heritage Making and Migrant Subjects in the Deindustrialising Region of the Latrobe Valley
Alexandra Dellios

Heritage and Design: Ten Portraits from Goa (India)
Pamila Gupta

Heritage, Education and Social Justice
Veysel Apaydin

Geopolitics of Digital Heritage
Natalia Grincheva and Elizabeth Stainforth

Here and Now at Historic Sites: Pupils and Guides Experiencing Heritage
David Ludvigsson, Martin Stolare and Cecilia Trenter

Heritage and Transformation of an African Popular Music
Aghi Bahi

The Neoliberalisation of Heritage in Africa
Rachel King

Will Heritage Save Us? Intangible Cultural Heritage and the Sustainable Development Turn
Chiara Bortolotto

In Search of National Ancestors: Heritage, Identity and Placemaking in China
Shu-Li Wang

AI and Image: Critical Perspectives on the Application of Technology on Art and Cultural Heritage
Anna Foka and Jan von Bonsdorff

Why Historic Places Matter Emotionally: Responses – Attachments – Communities
Rebecca Madgin

A Chinese Discourse of Heritage
Song Hou

A full series listing is available at: www.cambridge.org/CHSE

For EU product safety concerns, contact us at Calle de José Abascal, 56–1°, 28003 Madrid, Spain or eugpsr@cambridge.org.

www.ingramcontent.com/pod-product-compliance
Lightning Source LLC
LaVergne TN
LVHW011854060526
838200LV00054B/4325